SO MANY FRIENDS, SO
LITTLE FRIENDSHIP

SO MANY FRIENDS, SO LITTLE FRIENDSHIP

Imagine a world where so-called best friends are nothing but flakes!

AIGBEFO D. EHIHI

Aishific Press

Unless otherwise indicated, all Scripture quotations are taken from
the *Holy Bible*, New Living Translation, copyright © 1996, 2004, 2015
by Tyndale House Foundation. Used by permission of Tyndale
House Publishers, Carol Stream, Illinois 60188. All rights reserved.
Scripture taken from the King James Version of the Bible.
Scriptures taken from the Amplified Bible, Copyright © 1954, 1958,
1962, 1964, 1965, 1987 by The Lockman Foundation. They are used
with permission.
Scripture taken from the New King James Version®. Copyright ©
1982 by Thomas Nelson. Used by permission. All rights reserved.

ISBN: 979-8-9860-0170-8
Library of Congress Control Number: 2023906497

Published by Aishific Press.
Aishific Press
Visit www.aisificpress.com
books@aishific.com
1 (352) 300 6373

Printed and bound in the United States of America.
Revised Edition, 2023.

Contents

DEDICATION

This book is dedicated to my dearly departed mother,
Mrs. Yemisi Justina Ehihi.

ACKNOWLEDGEMENT

With all love and adoration, I appreciate my beautiful
wife, Precious, and my adorable daughter, Felicity,
for all their love and support. I also appreciate everyone
who has contributed to the success of this book.

INTRODUCTION

A friend loves at all times...

Show me your friends, and I will tell you who you are. I can remember my parents pounding that saying into my head over and over again. Unfortunately, we find ourselves in a generation where we are unreasonably judged by the value of our acquaintances, buddies, or so-called friends and neither by the content of our hearts nor our behavior alone. In a world where so-called best friends are nothing but flakes, we must wholly utilize *So Many Friends, So Little Friendship* as a tool for becoming and making a delightful friendship that will benefit us and others. Remember, you will continue to be the same person and remain in the same place for years to come, except for these two most important things: your circle of friends and your sources of information.

This book helps readers start thinking about those in their circle. It details how to make any significant changes to their friendship and how to be a true friend. It opens with the operational definition of friendship and continues on to introduce the perfect friend. The author discusses friendship, identifying friends and flakes, elements of true friendship, and how to be a true friend. The main goal of this book is to get you to start choosing the right friends. If you select your friends aimlessly, you may severely get hurt and may come to devastation. Still, a loyal and affectionate friend may be more reliable and connect more intimately than any family member (Proverbs 18:24). While you choose who should be your friend, the author introduces you to the One who is a perfect friend. Your life and relationship with others will never remain the same after consuming this book.

0 1

PONDER POINTS

> You will continue to be the same person and remain in the same place for years to come, except for these two most important things: your circle of friends and your sources of information.

One

FRIENDSHIP

Friends

The word *friend* has its deep origin in an Old English word, *frēond*, *frēon*, and *frend* (Middle English), which means to love. From the root, the word friend means loving and being loved. According to the Oxford English Dictionary, a friend is someone with whom you have mutual affection, typically platonic in nature, one exclusive of family relations. In other words, a friend should be attached to you by love, esteem, or an expected end. Considering different views of life, a friend could be seen as someone you love and who loves you as well. It may be that person you respect and who respects you too. It could also be someone with mutual trust. A friend should possess some shared understanding with you. They can be rich sources of social support in challenging times.[1] They can also be sources of stress themselves; it all depends on the quality of those in your circle of friends, how you relate with them, and how much of a good friend you are.

Friendship

Friendship has to do with mutual affection between two or more persons. It is more of a powerful bond or interpersonal relationship than a mere connection. Friendship has long been a prevalent study within psychology, sociology, philosophy, etc. Friendships are influential and potentially lifelong; they are elementary to our social, psychological, and physical well-being.[2] There are many forms of friendship. Some may vary from location to location. Some differ in behavioral order, and others in individual type. Some fundamental characteristics of friendship include altruism, trust, expression of one's feelings, shared understanding, affection, rituals, tenderness, sympathy, empathy, and the ability to articulate oneself without fear of judgment. Above all, love should be the pillar of friendship.

Cathy Mason asserts that friendship ostensibly requires viewing the other party as a person with fundamentally equal standing to oneself—and thus as someone whose overall mindset is prima facie dependable and worth taking seriously.[3] Even though there is no limit to the type of person to form a friendship, a friend still manages to share common goals, interests, backgrounds, occupations, and demographics. One thing that sets friendship apart is that it is an essential part of our daily social experience. It has across-the-board implications for our health and overall well-being.[4]

True Friendship

I see true friendship as a tremendous sensational exploit that guides the ongoing finding of oneself and one's friends. This can happen so that, after a while, if the friendship is nourishing, it becomes a quotidian expansion of one's perception of humanity. This creates opportunities for learning up to the minute about life, faith, and oneself, especially the human and scriptural way of living. The remarkable attribute of friendship, on which Mason focused her article, is that friends take one another thoughtfully.

Friends take one another's interests, projects, and beliefs as at least prima facie reasons to care, believe, and act similarly.[5] According to the sacred text, true friendship is characterized by love. The Book of Proverbs, the example of David and Jonathan in the book of 1 Samuel 18, and the instructions given to the church in the New Testament all portray the characteristics of true friendship. The perfect examples Jesus laid for us to follow provide a creative visualization of true friendship. True friends should be loyal, trustworthy, and transparent, no matter the situation.

True friends may not be perfect, but they always love, are loyal, forgive even when it seems impossible, and strive for the other's welfare. Your true friends are always meant to love no more, no less. They are liable to hurt us only in responsible ways, such as tough love. Most friends are more loyal than family members (Proverbs 18:24). True friends can provide and promote mutual edification, which sharpens the countenance of one's friends. The Sacred Scripture advises that he who walks with a wise man will be wise (Proverbs 13:20). The principal characteristic of a true friend is the willingness to make sacrifices for their friends when the need arises. As the author of John puts it, apart from Jesus, no one has ever shown more extraordinary love, especially to the point of laying down their life for their friend (John 15:13).

02

PONDER POINTS

I challenge you to take a momentous look at those in your friendship zone, and you will discover your life's direction lies there.

Two

WHO ARE YOUR FRIENDS?

> Birds of the same feather flock together in
> the same direction.

Who are your friends? This question may sound too familiar or too easy to answer. This old-time saying aligns with Proverbs 13:20: show me your friends, and I will tell you who you are. Before responding to the above question, I implore you to think deeply because you may not have previously comprehended the difference between authentic and fake friends. If I were to ask you this question in person, you might have many names or images to respond with. Some may be grouped as your "special friends," and some "casual friends," or you may even refer to some as just "friends." The truth is, these people in your life are either suitable for you or bad for you. In other words, they are either the right friends (real friends) or the wrong friends (flakes).

Before we continue, I am not trying to dissuade you from making friends. I desire that you make good friends. Research reveals that having fewer and lower-quality social relationships is associated with poorer physical health and a greater risk for early mortality. On the other hand, having more and better relationships is associated with better physical health and greater odds of survival.[6] My message is to ensure you keep better and quality relationships with people who care about you, as this can foster healthy relationships and good health. According to studies, a healthy relationship is one of the most significant factors for healthy living. We must comprehend the various implications of friendship and its consequences in our life. This is because positively influential associations can significantly pave the way for deleterious assimilation. So also, disreputable companionship will significantly contaminate a well-brought-up individual.

Let me also bring this to your understanding: you can never be different from your friends or the people you always hang out with. The words of my dearly departed mother, "Birds of the same feather flock together in the same direction," always echoed in my mind whenever I mingled with those she disapproved of. That saying is practically true. The friends we keep can be a significant factor in determining how great or insignificant one will become. The earlier you recognize this, the better because they impact your path to the top, no matter who you are, where you are, or what you aspire to become. Your future or destiny may be jeopardized if you have flakes disguised as your buddies, like wolves in sheep's clothing.

Trust me—friends will either influence you positively or negatively. They can launch you into the circle of great men or press you into the process of frustrated fellows, which I call the pit of life. Friends are significant factors that determine your success, especially whether you will ever fulfill your destiny and enjoy the fullness of the only life you've got to live. Be it good or bad friends, male or female, old or young, they may never stop influencing you as long as you are within their sphere of influence. The sad thing is that one can quickly imitate and adapt to their so-called friends' evil or sinful lifestyles.

An association can bring about assimilation. Punzo Valentina believes that the social norms of the social groups and their enforcement (through the process of deterrence) are the causally relevant social and environmental features. They determine the criminogenic exposure—that is, they are the moral context conducive to criminal activities.[7] It's shocking to discover that we unconsciously mimic people's behavior or idiosyncrasies soon after spending some time with them. Most times, we don't even have to be with them long enough before we start making hand gestures like them, saying their favorite clichés, or making facial expressions as they do. We, in essence, absorb and conform to our friends' behavior depending on our rate of exposure and self-control.

We are often ignorant of this because most of us live without paying attention to details—we must be observant enough to know what is happening. Most of us live carefree lives with an "I don't care" attitude. It is not forever straightforward to understand what type of relationship we are in most of the time—realizing whether someone is a friend or a flake is tough. This is primarily accurate if you pay less attention to details. We must always consider one prevailing conception of friendship: friendships are characteristically close, intimate, and trusting.

This very nature of friendship has led various recent philosophers to claim that friendship involves one's openness to having their character shaped by their friends.[8] The ability for friendship to be pe one's character is known as "friendship versus character-shaping risks." Mason further explains that merely because someone is one's friend, one risks becoming like them—concerning goodness, this seems to be an overstatement and plausibly a risk that one could guard against.[9] I encourage you always to do all you can to guard against the risk of becoming too similar to your friends. Also, regardless of the friendship, always retain some significant control over your character despite your friends' influence.

Here are selected tips you can use to evaluate the direction of your friendship. It is as simple as asking yourself these basic questions:

• Do your friends make you feel good?

• Do you ever wonder if your friends say negative things about you in your absence?

• Do your friends say negative things about other people behind them?

• Do your friends ever request you to do things you are uncomfortable with?

• Do your friends make you feel like you are not as good as they are?

• Do your friends dislike when you hang out with others without them?

• Do your friends ask you to contribute more to the relationship?

• Do your friendships make you feel safe and comfortable?

• How much do you trust your friends?

• How much do you think they believe you?

• What have you gained or lost so far in your friendship?

• Above all, does your friendship glorify God?

By examining yourself with these questions, you will start thinking critically about the kind of friends you've been keeping. After reading this chapter, you will know if keeping them in your life is worth it. While you are still asking and thinking about these questions, let me help you by differentiating between your good and wrong friends.

Flakes

An ungodly man unearths evil, and there is a blazing fire in their lips. An obstinate person sows strife, and a gossiper separates good friends. A fierce person lures their neighbor and ushers them in a way that is not good. They shut their eyes to conceive errant things; when they move their lips, they cause evil to reign (proverbs 16:26–30). Just as it sounds, a flake is a fake friend. They are primarily shady, deceitful, unreliable, selfish, and flaky. For the rest of this book, we will refer to bad friends as flakes. Longstanding research shows that these flaky characteristics are made either by choice, nature, or nurture. People in this category are feeble in heart, lacking discipline, self-control, morals, and salvation. They mostly become friends with people because of what they can benefit from them.

Things that easily attract flakes to your life are valuables, attention, fame, money, comfort, and convenience. It's not unusual to think poorly of people who befriend flakes. Societies tend to feel that friendship with flakes reveals something unattractive about otherwise good individuals. It makes one perturbed about them. Cathy Mason explains that a company with flakes seems to be morally troubling. She asserts that it is common to feel that those who are friends with people in this category may have made questionable choices in entering the relationship. This may explain why there's something morally wrong about simply being friends with a bad person.[10]

A flake's principal objective is all about them. They will cause you more grief, anger, and frustration than you can imagine. Flakes don't value those they associate with; they are the type that will run away from the accident scene. Flakes are superb at making plans and promises but need to improve at keeping them. Flaky friends may make their friends feel good in private, but in public, they will embarrass or make them look bad in the presence of others. They like taking advantage of their friends and will never see anything virtuous in their buddies. Flakes will severely demean your hard-earned accomplishments.

Flakes backbite, snitch, gossip, ridicule, and destroy those who regard them as their friends, especially in their absence. Flakes can be unstable like sea waves and manipulative, domineering, and erratic in relationships. They never admit their faults and may never feel remorse for their wrongdoings. Flakes are great pretenders who may not like seeing you succeed because they don't strive for success. They are phonies, and one needs to stay away from them. Like the devil, their mission in your life is to steal, kill, and destroy. They will not stop until they see you come to ruin. These people cannot keep a relationship due to their way of life. Question or advise them, and you will see how quickly and easily they'll get rid of you and move on to another ignorant and available person. In several places in the Scripture, they are called foolish, unreliable, ungodly, froward, etc. Unsurprisingly, Mason asserts that friendships with flakes risk one's moral character.[11] They entail risking one's character to be shaped in immoral ways per the friend's mistaken attitudes and ideals.

Mason is right, especially when the ways of bad friends are deceitful, regretful, and confusing. They mostly like associating with immoral and sinful things because that is where they derive their pleasure. They don't appreciate you in any definite form but instead, depreciate you in value. They do all they can to hold you at the bottom because they know there is no room for them if you reach the top. This is what is commonly known as a crab mentality. Just like a crab would, they have all the tools to distract you from your purpose in life. They may become a nuisance to your life and even cause you to be far from God. When you walk into a gathering of those kinds of people, you suffer from things you are not guilty of. You are judged and reprimanded in many ways because of your flaky companions. Think about those who are friends with viciously immoral and racist people. Mason made an excellent example.

> For example, news coverage of the disgraced financier Jeffrey Epstein, a sex offender revealed to have been involved in extensive sex trafficking, has suggested that his close friends were tainted too. Such reports implied something terrible about their being friends with him. Some of those cases are complicated by concerns that his friends were complicit in his wrongdoing or even active wrongdoers themselves. Still, even those who were not complicit in his wrongdoing seem somehow sullied by their friendship with him.[12]

Such friendships seem to reflect poorly on them. And think about it: the mere fact that one is in the circle of those with deeply immoral characters makes others feel uncomfortable around them. There is this proverbial warning my father always had me read as part of my scriptural memorization: don't befriend angry people or associate with hot-tempered people, or else you may find yourself learning so hard to be like them, which may severely jeopardize your essence. Don't forget that you will continue to be the same person and remain in the same place for years to come, except for these two most consequential things: your circle of friends and sources of information.

03

PONDER POINTS

If you walk with wise people, you will be
wise also, but if your companions are fools,
you may be destroyed with them.[13]
A person who lies down with dogs may
wake up with fleas.

Three

THE EFFECT OF FLAKY ASSOCIATION

> Do not be misled; corrupt communication
> pollutes pleasant manners.[14]

Bad friends are mostly concerned with the things that lead to destruction. The Bible always regards this set of people as wicked. They can initiate us into another purpose instead of our primary objective. This veers us from God's divine purpose for our life. Their ways are mostly filled with deceit and regrets. Like I said earlier, flakes delight in associating with sinful behaviors because that is where they derive pleasure. They don't appreciate us but relatively devalue us. Most flaky friends will do all they can to hold us down because they know there is no room at the top, and they don't want to feel lonely at the bottom. They have all it takes to distract you from your purpose in life. In many ways, they make us disadvantaged. They even make us far from God when we walk in their companionship. We suffer for things we are not guilty of; we are judged together in iniquity. And we are criticized because of the association we find ourselves in.

If one is not careful, flakes can make one forfeit their integrity. And when one has flakes as friends, they will not escape being judged by their friends' ways. Odious companions can occupy our hearts and disconnect us from God and His word. One may only experience progress in life if one abstains from flakes. As good friends can lead you into a satisfying relationship with God, a flake can lead you in many ways that are abominations to God. Friendship with flakes leads to moral failure and character destruction because friendship involves taking the other person's attitudes, beliefs, and endeavors seriously.

A deep friendship with a flaky person is naturally problematic, especially if you are still committed to following Christ daily. The author of Proverbs in the Holy Scripture explains that there are six things that the Lord hates. Yet, seven are an abomination unto Him: a proud countenance, a tongue that lies, a person that kills or destroys innocent people, a heart that instruments wicked imaginations, feet that are swift in wrongdoing, a fraudulent witness that speaks lies, and those that sow conflict among brethren—the Lord detests them all (Proverbs 6:17–19).

The proverb above warns that a flake's sinful ways may be an abomination unto God. You might happily say there are some things you usually do that were not mentioned in that passage. Suppose you or your friends are thieves, fornicators, gossipers, drug addicts, drunkards, gang members, murderers, jest makers, troublemakers, and so much more. In that case, your ways are an abomination to God. This is especially true when you are not trying to repent of your sins. It is even worse when you refuse to disassociate yourself from these evildoers you call your friends.

Several Scriptures, like the letter sent to the Thessalonians, urge us to "refrain from every sinful appearance" (2 Thessalonians 5:22). Many are suffering today; some rot in jail, some end up in prison, and some have been killed today, not because they were terrible people from the onset but because they suffer the sinister consequences of wrong association. Your so-called friend may ruin your life if you don't refrain from them. Some may only support you if it delights them. What ways could satisfy a vicious person? The ways that could satisfy a wicked person may be the patterns of monstrosity that may cast you into the abysmal pit of life. Some flakes are so self-centered that they believe the world only revolves around them.

Some may never look forward to any appropriate future ambition, vision, or hope for living; that is why some will make sure you lose yours too. Some so-called friends are too dangerous to be with because danger looms around them.

Some flakes may even offer to steal, lie, or kill for your sake, and those friends will never help you achieve anything good in life except to hurt someone to seek vengeance. May God deliver you from every unfriendly person in your life in Jesus's Name (Amen).

Some people can buy you smokes or alcoholic drinks to entertain themselves as you get messed up. They can pay for anything that will turn you up or things that may not be healthy for you. Still, they may never spend money on anything to help, empower, or raise you in the long run. Such so-called friends will buy you things that will satirize you so you can serve as a source of entertainment to them, especially in public places. They are ready to spend their last dollar to make you act silly, publicly and otherwise. Most times, some friends will tell you they want to take you out for a good time, and you may count it as an opportunity to enjoy yourself. This little enjoyment goes as far as denting your promising future.

Here is another warning from the Proverbs regarding these flakes: my dear, if wrongdoers tempt you, disagree. If they reached to you and said, come with us, let us stay here and wait for blood, let us lurk in privacy for the innocent without reason, do not walk in the path with them, abstain from their way (Proverbs 1:10–15). Their courses are too dangerous for you. I plead with you today, anytime you see this kind of person or so-called friends, all you need to do is to desert them. If you don't, they will deceive you into tainting your image. They might also draw you closer to Satan, your enemy, and your enemy will be so happy to mess you up. You may be thinking right now that you can change them. You should always pray for them but don't ever mistake that you can change them when you have already been contaminated.

There was this time in my life when I thought I could change my so-called friends. As I was trying to stop them from smoking, they were trying to teach me how to drink. Sometimes you may think you are changing them, but don't be surprised when you discover they have successfully changed you from whom you think you are. They will teach you their ways, and you will quickly learn, but they will say your ways are "too difficult" to follow, and you know it is easier to destroy than to build. Let me encourage you to start moving with people with the vision, future, ambition, drive, and above all, the love and passion for Christ. Apostle Paul warns the Thessalonians to abstain from all sinful appearances. If we refuse to be attentive to Apostle Paul's warning, we may begin to learn the ways of these flakes who parade themselves as friends. Let us discuss some things we may quickly adopt if we keep making companions with these flakes.

The Way They Talk

> The tongue can bring death or life; those who love to talk will reap the consequences (Proverbs 18:21).

We first want to discuss how flakes talk and how we start talking like them if care is not taken. The Bible warns extensively about how we speak, and the consequences if not controlled, are destructive. Some people enjoy having ill conversations about our political leaders, religious leaders, and maybe even those they seem to dislike. They may seem funny whenever they talk about others, but you must be careful about them. What usually comes out of their mouth is carnal, foolish, or mostly unrighteous talk. When flakes converse, they mostly gossip and backbite. Their conversation usually targets sensitive issues, leaders, religions, ladies, or great men of God. Remember, corrupt communication damages good behavior.

Your destiny matters so much that you don't have time for foolish talk. You may talk or behave foolishly like them if you are not careful enough to disconnect from such so-called friends. And it doesn't end there; you may start becoming as flaky as those you hang out with. Regardless of who you are with, you must never forget that it doesn't happen immediately. When the Bible says that evil communication corrupts good manners, it means it happens over time. The more you hang out with flakes, the more their conversation will corrode you—the flakier you become.

Their Behavioral Disorder

We often love some people because of their notorious behavior; those who always like this ill behavior seem to do so probably because of intimidation, low self-esteem, their environment, and home training. We also love their way of life because we think they may be trending, having fun, and saying, "It is my life, and I only have one time to enjoy it." Still, we must ask ourselves these questions: Where were the people who once behaved like this? Are they doing what their creator created them to do? Is it because we don't know who we are, or do we follow immoral paths to satisfy the fleshy desires that will lead us to destruction? These questions are critical to our friendship because the ways that seem fitting to an individual may be ways that lead to ruin.

Habits

It is not surprising that the behaviors of a flake sometimes entice us. Habits like lying, quarreling, gossiping, backbiting, drinking, smoking, masturbating, fornication, etc.—we imitate them anytime we see them manifesting. Even when we don't want to do some things we dislike, we see ourselves indulging in one of those habits because we associate with them. These are habits that were not part of us from the beginning. When there is a close relationship, there is always a rub-off of characteristics, patterns, attitudes, and behavior. Either you influence them, or they influence you, period. Still, instead of us influencing them, we end up under their influence, embracing whatever comes from them.

Character & Lifestyles

> *Good character guides true friendship,*
> *but dishonesty destroys relationships.*

Some people we call our friends, their character and lifestyle are nothing to write home about. The unrighteous thing is that we don't just admire them; we also emulate them. Sometimes the characters they struggle with are the ones we even imitate most. You may think their lifestyle is making waves for them, but do you think it is accepted reputably beyond reproach? Do you believe God will be happy that you are going astray in the way of the world? How long will you allow your so-called friends to continue to corrupt you? If you don't have anybody to advise you, why don't you counsel yourself so you can be more helpful in this life? What will you tell your generations to come? What justification will you present to your creator when you don't fulfill your purpose on earth due to the character and lifestyle you got from your so-called friends?

Our modern-day societies are looking for people of exemplary character to lead them. They want people responsible enough to reflect the excellent characteristics of a good leader. Will you now exempt yourself from being among the responsible ones just because your friends are ready to stop you from getting to your promised land? Apostle Paul's instruction on this subject is very detail oriented. He instructed that you should not become so modified by the behavior and customs of this world. He also warned against conforming to them without thoughtful consideration. Instead, you should focus your attention on God. Allow God to transform your life throughout, primarily how you process things. Readily realize what God wants from you and respond to it quickly. Unlike the behavior and customs around you, constantly yanking you down to their immaturity levels, God wants the best for you. He inspires you to be the best. He designs a well-developed maturity in you that helps you shine.

In my college days, I accommodated a brother who seriously needed accommodation. I empathized with him; we were both Christians from different backgrounds. I envied his Christian life; he seemed more fervent than I was. He spoke more tongues than I did when praying and quoted more Scriptures. As I got to know him more, I started to learn more about his hidden demeanor. Instead of rebuking those immoral behaviors, I blended into his immoralities. He ended up influencing me to a greater extent.

Most of our conversations became sinful by the day as they focused on women, sex talk, and the deficiencies among great men and women of God. Little did I know I was in the snare of destruction—because it was strange at first, but I became comfortable with it after a while. No wonder the Holy Book of Wisdom said the way that seems proper to you might be the way that ushers to ruin (Proverbs 14:12). When we were supposed to be in class, I joined him in playing games at the game houses because he was a game addict. The funniest thing was that I was never good at playing those games. But he would tell me not to worry and that I would get used to it.

I was trying to get used to it instead of focusing on my classes. Do you see the type of person I called a friend? It did not occur to me that I had started talking and behaving like him—and getting used to ladies. All these did not happen overnight; it took some time. I was going astray, back to my old ways of playfulness and unseriousness, until I failed my exams. It was painful, but I thanked God I discovered to recover myself early. So, will you wait until you fail before you retrace your footsteps? Please don't wait until it is too late. I pray that God will deliver you from every friendship that will ruin your destiny; God will open your eyes to be conscious of the danger of the types of friends you keep. This lets you let go of every unfriendly relationship as early as possible.

What They Call Fashion

> Beauty does not lie in the exposure of private parts, but in the eye of the beholder.

The way some of our so-called friends dress may sometimes portray a high level of irresponsibility. Our societies today judge us according to our dress; we are addressed based on our fashion choices. If you have been rejected due to your outfit (the way you dress), change your dress and dress more appropriately. Dress responsibly and see if you will not be ceremoniously accepted. Whether we like it or not, we will always be affected by how we dress the body God created. It speaks for us mostly when we dress ready for business. How we dress goes a long way to affect us in our presentation. It is always good to dress the way you want to be addressed. Exposing what is supposed to be private to the public portrays some levels of self-esteem issues. Beauty does not lie in the exposure of private parts but in the eye of the beholder.

Our first appearance matters most to people. So, if you dress inappropriately, you may be addressed as such. You may even attract inappropriate comments. When you dress appropriately, you will be reputed above your status. Some of our body parts must be beautifully concealed and only seen by our appropriate intimate partners. Abstain from those that dress seductively. Seductive or revealing fashion trends are strongly motivated by immorality. A Christian shouldn't be imitating such immoral tendencies. Remember, Christians must learn to abstain from every appearance of sinful behaviors. Let your spirit and soul be happy you are caring for the body, properly covering every part that doesn't need public exposure.

Dress the body in an appreciating manner and see whether God will not update you by crowning you. From these few points I have given, you will discover that you have been flocking with the wrong friends if all they follow is trending immoral fashion. One thing I want to remind you of is that it is never too late to have a change of heart. As friends, we are supposed to imitate positive behaviors of each other. Your friends are meant to edify you with the good news and share your pain and burden. We need to keep friends that please God so our ways are right with God. When our habits are right with God, He will cause our enemy to be at peace with us. We all need friends who will lead us to greatness, inspire us to fulfill our life purpose and ameliorate us to be fit for the kingdom. As you read, more emphasis will be placed on this further in the chapter.

Once again, I ask, who are your friends? Remember, God warns us against the paths of these wicked friends, especially through the passage that says you should not enter the crooked path of the wicked. And go not in the way of immoral people. Avoid it, do not pass by it, turn from it, and abstain from it completely. They sleep not unless they have caused misconduct; they will lose sleep unless they cause you to fail. They eat the bread of wickedness and drink the wine of violence, but the paths of the just are the shining light that shineth more and more until the perfect day (Proverbs 4:14–17).

If you want to be a wise man, you will avoid flakes at all costs or risk learning their hateful and wicked habits until you destroy yourself. They will make you lose your integrity, self-esteem, and respect. When your friends are sorry, you cannot escape being judged by their ways. You can never move forward in life if you don't run away from those kinds of people.

As you read this book, many people are suffering—some are in jail, some are on death row, some have been killed, some are about to die, and some have serious diseases. Some are under the wrath of God. This is not necessarily because they are bad or planned it that way, but primarily because of the flakes in their lives; they received a judgment they did not deserve. Most of your so-called best friends will ruin your life, marriage, blood, sweat, and tears if you don't withdraw from them.

I advise you to examine your life comprehensively and use this book as an antivirus to eradicate the flakes in your life. Those who walk with righteous persons will be righteous, and those who befriend one with wisdom from above will be wise. Still, a friend of fools will face a devastating end. You might want to say this author is too harsh on this issue; it is all for your good. It is worth it; seeing this book impact your life is my greatest joy. Your future is too bright to be messed up just like that. Do not let anybody in the disguise of love drag your flight to the land of fulfillment. You cannot continue with those flakes at the bottom of the ladder.

If you are there wondering how to make a change, Christ is one true and perfect friend who is always ready to help you find other good friends like Him. He happily welcomes you onboard to the flight that will soar you to greater heights in life. The time has come for you to be skyrocketed to the top by that "perfect friend." He is better than you, knows more than you, and will give you a new identity. I will put more emphasis on this perfect friend in the chapters to come.

04

PONDER POINTS

Since only a few people have experienced true friendship in the course of their life, very few value it. The more value you put into any relationship, the more work you will put into it.

Four

TRUE FRIENDS

How Do You Recognize a True Friend?

C.S. Lewis saw friendship as the love that is dismissed, a rare gem, the crown of life, and the school of integrity that the modern world ignores. He claimed friendship seemed the cheeriest and most effusive of all loves. Lewis asked why the contemporary world disregards the beauty and virtue enveloped in friendship. It could be because we all know true friendship is laborious, rarely celebrated, and the one form of relationship we believe we could live without. It could also be that, as Lewis puts it, "since only a few experience true friendship, very few value it." [15] A fling may lend itself to conception, love stimulates a sense of belonging, and our friendliness provides a track to revitalization. But friendship offers a different productivity rate than that of a consumer mindset.

However, Lewis believes friendship may likely have the most immediate likeness to Heaven, where we will be entwined in our affinities. Since we develop relationships over something in common, that longing for companionship makes us want more genuine friendship. Friendship must be about something, even if it is only an enthusiasm for a game or hobby. "Those with nothing cannot share anything. Those traveling nowhere can never have fellow travelers." [16] This brings us to the truth about friendship: friendships have started movements, shaped fundamental beliefs, and contributed to numerous undertakings, from craftwork to trading to building empires.

A true friend happens to be someone who doesn't care about your looks. They don't care about how boring you may be; surprisingly, most don't even think about it. They are friends who will forgive you no matter what you do. They may attempt to help you even when they don't know how. They may also be someone who tells you if you're acting stupid but doesn't make you feel asinine. A true friend is very challenging to find. As we age, we see ourselves drifting away from those we've always known to be our best friends. This is especially true for those friends you made during childhood, teenage years, and even during high school and college days. It can be challenging to find new friends now and then. Maintaining old relationships may be even more demanding as we undergo various stages of life. You are fortunate if you are serendipitous enough to find true friendship in your life. This is because most of us make a great effort daily to adjust and find one true friend that is real and consistent.

What Can You Look Out for in a True Friend?

A true friend loves unconditionally through thick or thin. A true friend does not betray the trust of friends, irrespective of the situation, even if it will benefit them—someone who knows you better than you can ever imagine and takes a position in your best interest in a time of crisis. True friends influence those they associate with to be like or better than them. True friends don't get jealous when they see their friends with others. They don't envy the success of their friends; instead, they strengthen, encourage, and admonish one another to achieve their goals. They don't force themselves on someone or cause someone to become their friend.

The life of a true friend is just like the one of Jesus Christ, who has given everyone the perfect opportunity to become one of His friends. He keeps His promises and always tells the truth regardless of what may happen at that particular time. Christ is His word, which means everything to Him as He is committed to His word.

Who Are Your Friends?

Real friends are faithful to their word, and when they give you their word, they don't contradict it—i.e., everything you say should be a bond. True friends will never engage in malicious talk, gossip, or abusively disparaging speech behind their buddies. They communicate openly, making each other aware of their anger, wrongs, displeasure, grievances, expectations, etc. They address their differences as quickly as possible and amicably within themselves, given no room for malice. With true friends, your secret will always remain your secret. With all these, are real friends perfect? No, they are not; they only strive for perfection in response to God's Word.

I learned recently that friendship cannot be found on the side of the road. Nor can it be gifted by someone. It is a process that goes on as you walk through life. It is not a gift; it is a reward. It is an achievement of your goodness, unending sacrifices, and unwavering commitment. It is a feeling that gives you strength, and it is always with you wherever you go. It makes your happiest moment more comfortable and your saddest moment lighter. Your real friends will love you for who you are, in the good and bad times. They can find out about your past and still love you. They are always there to listen to you, whether you need to talk, cry, or even sing. They will never tell your secret to anyone unless keeping it will endanger your life. They can be truthful with you regardless of the situation, even at the risk of hurting your feelings. They are friends who can sometimes disagree with you and remain good friends; otherwise, they cannot be called true friends.

They will never gossip about you. Instead, you and your privacy will always be relevant to your buddies. They also stick by you no matter what it will cost them unless you've done them some wrong that can harm their destiny or future. They don't disappear from your life without good reasons. They adore being nearest to you as much as it is feasible, at least by heart. True friends do anything for you unless it is unreasonable for them to do it. They are friends with kind hearts and always hold their friends close to them.

True friendship is not always sweet and rosy. True friendship is not a no-conflict relationship but one that compromises on the essentials and may conflict with the nonessentials. They are human; they are imperfect beings, and they make mistakes. They can also hurt you the most because they know everything about you. The good thing is that when they hurt you, they don't just leave you hanging; they will certainly apologize if they have wronged you and consistently devise plans to make it up to you or make you feel better.

Your real friend is someone you may not see or hang out with for months or longer, but when you finally meet again, it's like those months never happened. They don't always have to be by your side for you to feel you both understand each other. They could be better, but they cover you as much as possible. I always refer to them as the transcendent kind of friends. They don't sugarcoat essential things like that because they care about your well-being, even though they present things unconventionally. Real friends will watch you dance like a maniac in public but eventually join you because they don't want you to look like a lunatic alone. They will love you and say it at random times. They are the type that will still be by your side decades from now. You will be old and wrinkled, but you will still be lifelong partners. They listen to your every word, never interrupting you, no matter how long or irrelevant your complaints may be.

Lastly, a true friend calls you now and then, asks you how

you are doing, and tells you how much you mean to them, no matter the situation, either directly or indirectly. As the famous saying goes, a friend that sticks with you in time of need is a friend indeed. Such friends can never be replaced, not even with hundreds of people, no matter how beautiful, good-looking, wealthy, or sweet-talking the temptation. This is a scriptural description of such friends; a friend clings tighter than a brother or sister (Proverbs 18:24b). With love, true friendship makes two souls become one, so they can often sense what the other person thinks or feels.

Many marriages are based on this kind of friendship, which lasts through the trials and tribulations a relationship may experience. Unsurprisingly, the Psalmist started the Psalms with advice for companionship. As the Psalmist puts it, the person who does not follow the path of sinners or sit in the company of fools is divinely blessed. And if they delight in the Lord's Word and meditate on it day and night, they shall be like a tree planted by the river. They shall yield fruit in and out of season, their leaf will never wither, and whatever they do will flourish (Psalms 1:1–3).

05

PONDER POINTS

People will always say, "Blood is thicker than water" when choosing family over friends, but Jonathan even turned his back on his father for his friendship with David. In other words, this type of friendship is "thicker than blood" and "dearer than a brother."

Five

WHAT DOES THE SCRIPTURE SAY ABOUT FRIENDSHIP?

> If friends are chosen aimlessly, an individual will be severely hurt and may come to devastation. Still, a loyal and affectionate friend may be more reliable and connect intimately more than any family member.

One will ask questions like the following: What exactly is the Bible's perspective on friendship? The Bible, the written form of God's Word, is a living manual for every Christian, but do Scriptures tell us how to choose our friends? Where can we find references for friendship in the Holy Book? How can we be true friends to others? Furthermore, lastly, how do we express love to one another if we must do it in ways that please God? It is good to be inquisitive about questions like these. Inquisitiveness is the mother of any invention. Let me inform you that they are all vital issues that demand you to research the Bible to answer them spiritually and truthfully. I want to leave you with some verses and examples to satisfy your curiosity. I am sure these great scriptural verses will speak and enhance your understanding of the prominent subject of friendship.

Starting with Christ's words, "This is My commandment that you love and unselfishly seek the best for one another, just as I have loved you. No one has greater love and stronger commitment than Christ, who laid down his own life for his friends. You are my friends if you keep on doing what I command you. I do not call you servants any longer, for the servant does not know what his master is doing, but I have called you My friends because I have revealed everything I have heard from My Father" (John 15:12–15, AMP). There are several words of wisdom on friendship that applies to any relationship. Study and meditate on all these Proverbs to clearly understand the friendships that please God. The Book of Wisdom warns us not to make friends with angry people. It is better to stay away from a furious person (Proverbs 22:24). As I have discussed earlier, friends love through all kinds of weather, and families may stick together in all kinds of trouble (Proverbs 17:17). Faithful are the wounds of a friend who corrects out of love and concern. However, the kisses of an enemy are deceitful because they serve their hidden agenda (Proverbs 27:6). But there is a faithful and loving friend who is reliable and sticks closer than a brother (Proverbs 18:24).

Again, the Holy Book of Wisdom warns us never to abandon our friends or our family friends at any time. And when we are in trouble, a neighbor nearby is better than a relative far away (Proverbs 27:10). Whoever walks with the wise becomes wise. Still, the companion of fools will suffer harm (Proverbs 13:20). A person with too many friends will be broken in pieces and come to ruin, so choose wisely (Proverbs 18:24). Oil and perfume make the heart glad; so does the sweetness of a friend's counsel that comes from the heart (Proverbs 27:9). A perverse person stirs up conflict, and a gossip separates close friends (Proverbs 16:28). Whoever would foster love covers over an offense, but whoever repeats the matter separates close friends (Proverbs 17:9).

Through thick and thin, tall and short, big and small, and fast and slow, who do you think will always be there for you? It will be your best friend for sure. If you have one, do not let go. I know you must have met and known diverse people in your life. Most of them may be someone you know slightly but not a close friend, while others, you might consider friends. There may be only a few that you would find close as genuine friends, and that person may be closer to you than any immediate family member. Brother James, the brother of Jesus, warns Christians never to make friends with the world. He asked, Do you not know that friendship with the world (anything that does not glorify God) is enmity with God? Therefore, whoever wishes to be a friend of the world makes himself an enemy of God (James 4:4).

Through these Bible passages, true friends are those we can trust. They are those we can open our hearts to and share our visions and dreams without doubt or fear. A true friend is always there for the good and bad times, someone who will not abandon or desert you when the going gets tough. A true friend withstands the test of time, which is rare. Friends always come and go, but to have an accurate, lifelong, close personal friendship is truly a great blessing from God alone. Now that we have been proficient enough to ascertain what we mean by friendship, flakes, and true friendship, let's look at some examples set before us by the Holy Book. Since we are children of God, it will be advantageous to emulate the sacred Scriptures regarding how to live and whom to share our lives with. As a good practice, let us start with the friendship between our heavenly father and the father of all nations (God and Abraham).

God and Abraham
(Faith, Obedience, and Reward)

The relationship between God and Abraham involves faith through obedience. The Bible clearly states (2 Chronicles 20:7) that Abraham was God's friend. Prophet Isaiah also asserts in his records (Isaiah 41:8) that Abraham was a friend of God. James, a servant of God and the Lord Jesus Christ confirmed God's and Abraham's friendship in his epistle. James confirmed this when he said Abraham believed God, and God credited his faith to him as righteousness per His will; for this reason, Abraham was called God's friend (James 2:23).

Their friendship was bounded by endless faith, sacrifice, and obedience. The Bible did not portray Abraham as sinless in all forms and fashion, but Abraham's unending belief in God to lead his life, family, and properties made him exceptional. As seen in several accounts in the Bible, Abraham took delight in obeying the voice of God, regardless of the sacrifices involved. Please don't get it twisted; though Abraham was a friend of God, he did not get his salvation through his works but through his obedience and faith in the promise of God. Apostle Paul defined this well in the epistle to the Romans to clarify that salvation is offered through the gospel of Jesus Christ alone.

Humanly speaking, what shall we say that Abraham, our forefather, has found? Did he obtain a favored standing? I don't think so. This is because if Abraham was justified or acquitted from the guilt of his iniquities by the great things he did, he has something to boast about, but not before God. But what does the Scripture say about this? Abraham was full of faith, especially in how he firmly trusted God, and it was ascribed to him as righteous standing with God (Romans 4:1–3).

The fantastic thing about this friendship was that Abraham's firm reliance on God attracted an incentive from God. He was blessed beyond curse, and his blessing was spread for generations and generations to come. He experienced a miracle that surpassed medical and human understanding. As a result of his obedience to God, he found favor in the sight of God to be made the father of all nations, even though he had no child by then. In most cases, we claim the blessings of Abraham, but are we ready to apply for the responsibility of faith in God as Abraham did? If you are already working on this path of faith and obedience to God, I promise you that there is always a reward for the righteous, both earthly and heavenly.

The Genuine Friendship Between Jonathan and David (Altruistic and Lifesaving Relationship)

The genuine friendship between Jonathan and David can be seen as self-sacrificing and noble in nature. As you read about this friendship in the passage in 1 Samuel 18–20, you will find that they share much in common. Some problematic situations could have easily foiled their relationship; instead, they strengthened their friendship. From the story, we can see the connection between King Saul (the first king of Israel), Prince Jonathan (King Saul's Son), and David (the shepherd boy).

It was part of tradition for Jonathan to be the next king of Israel. King Saul disobeyed God, and as a consequence of his disobedience, the kingdom was taken away from King Saul forever. David, without asking, found favor in the sight of God. He was chosen to be the next king of Israel. The alarming success of David and his men in putting an end to the constant oppression from the Philistines gave rise to suspicion and jealousy from Saul. This brought enmity between King Saul and David, making Saul seek David's life.

There was this beautiful day: David was returning from destroying the Philistine, and on their way home, they were celebrated by the women. These women went out of all the cities of Israel, dancing and singing to meet King Saul with songs of joy, tambourines, and musical instruments. They played their musical instruments and danced while singing, "Saul has slaughtered his thousands, and David has slaughtered his ten thousand." The music from these women displeased Saul, so he became furious. Saul then said to himself, "My people have ascribed to David ten thousand, but they have only ascribed a thousand to me, their king." He asked himself, "What more can David have except the kingdom?" From then onward, Saul became jealous of David and suspicious of his every move (1 Samuel 18:6).

We could say that Jonathan discerned that David would be the succeeding king instead of him, the prince, but he made a friendship and loved David anyway. Apparently, the prince was inclined to trust God's choice of the next king, with a reasonable understanding that the same God chose his father over others. This also insinuates Jonathan's acceptance that he would never be king, and his household also may become subject to David when he becomes king. There were some positions where Jonathan had the opportunity to eliminate David, as some of us would, but he chose otherwise.

Saul instructed his servants and Jonathan, his son, to eradicate David. On the other hand, Jonathan, due to his strong attachment to David, told David about his father's atrocious plan for him. Jonathan cautioned David to find concealment in the fields the following morning. Jonathan promised to change his father's mind by talking to him about David. He promises to tell David everything he can find out about his father's plot if he cannot get him to change his mind. Jonathan told his father about David the following day, recounting all the lovely things about David.

Jonathan advised his father that the king must abstain from transgressing against his maid David, significantly when he has never harmed him. Jonathan also recounted how David has always assisted his father in any way possible. He even reminded him about when David endangered his life to extinguish Goliath, the giant of the Philistines, and how the Lord used him to bring all of Israel a great victory. He told the father, You were delighted in him then. He ended the father-and-son conversation with a question: Why should you annihilate a blameless man like David when there is no justification for this kind of action at all? After listening to Jonathan, Saul pledged that as long as the Lord lives, David will not be murdered (1 Samuel 19:1–6).

Jonathan chose to save David's life. At that time, he did his best, as he promised David, to talk to his father to restore their relationship. And from the Scripture above, we can see that he succeeded in convincing his father to pledge never to exterminate David. Many times afterward, the king strived to slay David; instead, Jonathan always aided his escape. There was a time when it became apparent to Jonathan that his father would do anything to kill David; Jonathan had to endanger his own life to defend his friend. Jonathan even went as far as confronting his frightful father regarding David, and his father's wrath was twirled toward him. Even though they went their separate ways, their separation was out of necessity in the long run. Even when they had to separate, Jonathan told David to go in peace because they had pledged allegiance to each other in the name of the Lord. God was the eyewitness of the sealant between them and their offspring perpetually.

They pledged to remain loyal to each other, including their households and kingdoms. The Scripture below shows that their covenant relationship is an excellent example of friendship that should be emulated. Jonathan requested that David treat him with his unchanging love for the Lord as long as he lives. Jonathan said, "If I die, please may you treat my lineage with this endless love, even when the Lord eliminates all your adversaries from the surface of the earth." So, Jonathan completed a weighty treaty with David by saying, "May the Lord eliminate all your adversaries," and Jonathan made David reestablish his solemn pledge of friendship again. It was accounted for Jonathan in the Scripture that he loved David as he loved himself. This is what true friendship is all about (1 Samuel 20:14–17).

After the separation, David was heartbroken to hear of his beloved friend's death. It was a vast and notable loss for David to hear the news of Saul and Jonathan's loss of life. He expressed his unpleasant emotions by composing a song to express his grief, titled "The Song of the Bow," and ensured the music was taught to everyone in Judah. I see this as a breathtaking accolade to a real friend, as many of us would have celebrated and shown gratitude to God for the death of our enemies. The record of David and Jonathan's genuine friendship and unwavering character has been preserved as precious lessons in the Bible for our benefit.

It shows the close affinity between the Father and Christ, the Son. They both prefer that exact, close, intimate relationship with everyone, including you. This sweet and unending friendship will remain a lasting legacy till the end of time. I believe that when they see each other at the resurrection party, their company will continue right from where it had stopped, and they may enjoy their blissful friendship for eternity. Do you know that you can also cultivate a friendship like that of Jonathan and David with Christ and those who share the same aspirations, goals, and dreams? I urge you always to consider finding mutual ground in friendship because it fosters your desired relationship.

In summary, the friendship between Jonathan and David is altruistic and lifesaving, and it can be used to sculpt one's relationship with others. Now we can understand where the ponder point came from. We claim "blood is thicker than water" when choosing family over friends, but we can see from the story how Jonathan even turned his back on his father for the sake of the love he shared with his friend. In other words, this type of friendship is "thicker than blood" and "dearer than a brother or sister." These men were practical and keen to show deep love for one another, exemplifying a genuine and lasting friendship.

Most of all, David and Jonathan were prepared to lay aside their lives for one another. Their connection was so pronounced in some of their valedictions. Jonathan offered his servant his weapons and instructed him to take them to the city. The moment the servant left, David got up, fell on his face, and bowed three times to the ground to portray respect and submission. After this, they grieved together and kissed, but David lamented more (I Samuel 20:41).

How often can you find this nature of friendship in this world full of flakes? The great news is that you may also be destined to have this relationship with Christ. Christ commands us to love and desire the best for one another unselfishly, just as he unconditionally loved you. No one has ever shown greater love or more substantial commitment (not to mention the extent of laying down one's life) for their friends. Christ said the only way to be His friend is to keep doing what He asked of you. This is why Christ will not call us servants anymore. The servant knows nothing about what his master does.

Christ calls us His friends because He sees us as friends and has disclosed everything He has heard from His Father, God (John 15:13–15). Secondly, with Christ being your friend, He will guide and direct your path to those like him (hope, vision, and drive) because likes attract likes. Christ in you is the hope of glory, getting new friends, and becoming a true friend to others. Lastly, a true friendship like that of David and Jonathan will last. Searching for a true friend and becoming a real friend will help you find common ground when discussing friendship.

Ruth and Naomi
(A Bittersweet Commitment)

This story connotes a painful commitment that leads to a delightful experience through patience. It all started with a family marriage relationship: Ruth's dear departed husband was Naomi's son, and we could tell they were also friends from the story. Naomi tried to convince Ruth to return home since the family bond was no longer there. On the other hand, Ruth was firm on her vow to return with Naomi to her native land in Israel; meanwhile, Ruth's friendship bond was unwavering. It was true that Ruth had suffered the loss of her husband, but she was not willing to also lose her dear friend, Naomi. Eventually, Ruth and Naomi returned home together, grief-stricken and traumatized.

The Bible recorded that they were devoted and truthful to one another. As a result of her truthfulness and commitment to Naomi, Ruth found favor and love in the sight of Boaz, Naomi's relative. Ruth and Boaz's union brought peace of mind and a source of pleasure to the life of Ruth and Naomi. The exciting part of this friendship is that Jesse came out of it. Jesse gave birth to David, and from David were twenty-eight generations to the time of Jesus, according to the record of Matthew. From the time of Abraham to David are fourteen generations. Between David's time and Babylon are fourteen generations, and there are fourteen generations from Babylon to the time of Christ (Matthew 1:17).

I appreciate this story so much that I tell it often because it portrays the reward of a devoted and sincere friend. It is delightful to know that our Lord and Savior came out of the lineage of Ruth. Imagine if Ruth had not followed Naomi back to her people; maybe she would not have enjoyed the peace of mind at the end, or perhaps she wouldn't be anywhere in the history or lineage of Jesus Christ. Most of the time, not all that sparkles can be regarded as gold, and not all gold will shine brightly, not even in flashing light, especially in its crude form. It's always advisable to seek God's guidance to know whom to be committed to. This is so that we will not miss what is destined for us, as the case of Ruth and Naomi portrays.

06

PONDER POINTS

Stop trying to change others as you wish,
since even you cannot fashion yourself the
way you want, because only God can alter
a man's heart.

Six

FOUR STEPS TO CHOOSING THE RIGHT FRIENDS

> Being a true friend to others will pave the way for
> excellence in your leadership, especially when you
> influence them positively.

Love Yourself

You must love yourself before you can even think of loving somebody else. And if you love yourself, you must care for anything that has to do with yourself and your future. You must also feel good about yourself, as this will reveal your love for yourself. It is of great necessity to realize that when you feel good about yourself, you will allure and evince the excitement of your being even more. You must egoistically seek your inner joy because this is the most substantial gift you can give anyone. Unless one is full of this unspeakable joy, one will have nothing to offer, as it is practically impossible to give out what you don't have. The Scripture says, "Love your neighbor as you love yourself." This means you must love and appreciate yourself as God's beautiful creature; this is an act of obedience to God's command and a step to fulfilling His purpose for your life.

The best way to start is to value yourself as you want to be respected. The knowledge you have about yourself will significantly influence how you love yourself. As David, the psalmist, mentioned, I will praise Him for how He has fearfully and wonderfully created me. Marvelous are the works of God in my life, and my soul knows it right well (Psalms 139:14). This text helps you understand that you are not ordinary; God created you to be unique as He wonderfully created you. You must always appreciate God's incredible artistry, making you who you are today. Here is another Scripture describing you: "But you are a chosen generation, a royal priesthood, a holy nation, a peculiar people; that you should show forth the praises of God who hath called you out of darkness into His marvelous light" (1 Peter 2:9).

I am confident that when you better perceive who you are (of God), you will have no option but to love yourself. The second greatest commandment in the Bible is the one of love. Appreciate God for creating you by loving yourself as a beautiful creature. Make Him happy for creating you in His image by taking good care of yourself. Your expectations in life depend on lots of things but mostly on you. You may succeed if nobody else believes in you, but you will never achieve anything or forgive yourself if you don't believe in yourself. You will need to change how you see yourself because when the image (or how you see yourself) is modified, it will dramatically change your performance, and whatever you attached to the words "I am," you will become. In other words, you should creatively visualize yourself as a winner, as that will unfathomably contribute to your success. Celebrated living always starts with that creative visualization of your aspiration. It is your creative aspiration held in your imagination that manifests itself in your relationships. Start believing in yourself. Love yourself. See yourself positively. Your positivity will help you seek positive relationships.

Examine Yourself

To have the right friends, you will need to examine yourself. What qualities would you not want to see in a friend, and are you sure you are not guilty of those things? Let us not deceive ourselves here. As regards the above statement, the Bible urges you to "examine yourselves, whether ye be in the faith; prove yourselves. Know ye, not yourselves, how that Jesus Christ is in you, except ye be reprobates" (11 Corinthians 13:5). You will need to choreograph yourself and do what you want to see in another person; behave the way you would like others to act. If you do what you like to see in others, you will attract the right friends to you. Remember what the law of attraction says: like attracts like.

My point here is that if positivity is the rudiment of your attitude when anticipating and envisaging enjoyment, gratification, and happiness, you will allure and build people, create situations, and promote events that uphold your unequivocal expectations. Those you attract into your life today are because of your lifestyle, character, and habits. And this has gone a long way in explaining that being compulsively eye-catching is about living a life that feels splendid to you. It's a complete transformation from the inside.

You will mainly attract most things in tip-top condition when you feel delightful about yourself, and it will be easy to set up circumstances in your life that work loveliest for you. In other words, you don't only attract those things that you are optimistic about or wish for yourself; you also attract the people and environments that match how you're operating and showing up in the world. Most of us vigorously chase after those we desire, and some naturally attract what we want. When we start living a life that feels most appealing to us, it is natural that we become more like the things we want to attract. For example, if you're going to experience happiness, be happy. If kindness is what you desire from people, then be kind first. If you want more honor from others, give honor to people. As regards this subject, let me tell you how I view this world.

The world is like a mirror that reflects the exact picture of who you are. If you think you are loving, friendly, and helpful, the world will reflect love, friendship, and help in return. And if you are full of hatred, wickedness, and evil, guess what: this mirror will reflect hatred, wickedness, and evil. Your world reflects who you are and what you give. If you change your way of living today, expect a change in the type of friends you will attract. You must be ready to change your old habits and repent of your old lifestyle to attract the right friends. After repenting your old ways, here is the good news. If you should be in Christ, you are a new creature: the old things have become your past; behold, all things become new in your life (11 Corinthians 5:17).

All things, including your friends, will become new. This may not happen automatically; you may have to work it out by making drastic decisions regarding your new life in Christ. If you are not thinking of changing your life pattern for a better one, you shouldn't even think of changing another person because a blind man cannot lead a blind man in the right direction. However, if you are ready to make a new beginning in your life today, I assure you that Christ has been waiting for this opportunity to turn your life around and help you experience a unique and fulfilled life. Since you have been reading and (hopefully) examining yourself simultaneously, we have seen that all Christ needs to help us live right is the opportunity to prove Himself in our life. As we proceed to the next step, we will get a clearer understanding of why we need the help of Christ in our friendship.

Acknowledge God

Lean on, trust in, and be confident in the Lord with all your heart and mind, and do not rely on your insight or understanding. Know, recognize, and acknowledge Him in all your ways, and He will direct and make your paths straight and plain (Proverbs 3:5–6). God wants to always play a role in every situation you find yourself in. What role do you think God always loves to play? It is a function of direction. He will never hesitate to direct your path if you play your part in acknowledging Him. God desires us to always place Him first in all we do because there is nothing you can do in this life that will be successful without God. You must be acquainted with His ways and direction to always benefit from His wisdom and guidance. Indeed, you will appreciate life more when you do anything under God's leadership.

As you continue reading this chapter, you will discover that Jesus Christ is the only perfect friend; He is the only one who can guide us through life's journey. He also knows the heart of everyone. Unless you are deceiving yourself, you cannot understand what is going on in the heart of another person, no matter how long you've known each other. "The heart of a man is deceitful above all things and desperately wicked: who can know it? I, the Lord, search the heart; I try the reins even to give every one according to their ways and according to the fruit of their doings" (Jeremiah 17:9–10).

This part of the Scripture helps us understand that He knows the heart of everyone. He will always lead you in the right direction. No wonder the psalmist said God leads him in the pathway of righteousness for God's namesake (Psalms 23:3). God promises that if we depend on Him each day, He will ensure we are always on course. He will approve as he deems fit to preserve all our footsteps. That's why it was said in one of his sayings that we should commit our work unto Him, and our thoughts will be established. This was David's prayer: Lead me, oh Lord, in your righteousness because of my enemies; make your way straight before my face (Psalms 5:8). David prayed this prayer because he was convinced that God could show him what to do, so he would always consult God before taking any step in his life.

Why Do We Need to Involve Him in Everything We Do?

Too often, we may foolishly think we are competent enough to make wise choices without involving God. We reason, "If God gave us a brain, why is it so important to ask him for help or directions in making our decisions?" The answer becomes apparent as we understand who God is and how and why He invented us. He knows us better than we do. Life will be better if we fully acknowledge God, just as David has shown us in this part of the Scripture (Psalms 139:1–16). It will gladden my heart to see you meditate on this, put yourself in the place of David, and make this prayer with a genuine heart.

You have scoured me, Lord, and know everything about me. You know, when I sit and rise, you observe every one of my thoughts from a distance. You detect my path going out and lying down; you know all my ways. Even though my word is still unuttered, Lord, you understand it completely. You surrounded me from every angle of life and laid your hand upon me. Such infinite knowledge is too magnificent for me and too giant to accomplish. Where can I ever go from your Spirit? Where can I ever flee from your presence? If I reach the heavens, you are there; even if I make my bed in the depths, you are always there. If I upsurge on the wings of the sunrise, dwell on the far side of the sea, even there, your hand will direct me, and your right hand will hold me.

If I say, "Surely the darkness will shroud me, and the light becomes dark around me," even the darkness will never be dark; the night will shine to you like the day, as darkness is a shining light to you. You did form my innermost being. You knit me together in my mother's womb. I will forever confess your praise because you have fearfully and wonderfully made me; your works are so beautiful; I know that right well. When I was made in the secret place, my frame was not a secret to you. I was knit together in the depths of the earth. Your eyes saw my body without a definite shape; all the days you predestined for me were penned in your book even before one of them existed (Psalms 139:1–16).

How precious to me are your thoughts, oh God? How vast is the sum of them? If I were to count them, they would surely be more numerous than grains of sea sand. When I awake, I can count till eternity; I will still be with you. God, if only you would eliminate the wicked, and those who are bloodthirsty speak of you with wickedness in their heart; your enemies misuse your name. Do I not hate those who hate you, Lord, and detest those who defy you? I have absolute hatred for them; I count them as my enemies. Search me, God, and know my heart; try and understand my impatient thoughts. See if there is any wicked and offensive way in me and lead me in the way everlasting. God is in control of everything that happens. He is the all-mighty God. He is the Sovereign Lord, and nothing is too hard for Him. He made the heavens and the earth with His great power and outstretched arm.

He rewards each person according to their conduct and as their deeds deserve. He desires the best for us. For this reason, He gave His only begotten Son to us as the perfect friend who can help us with real friends that can be an instrument to our uplifting. He who did not spare his own Son but gave him up for us all—how will he not also graciously give us all things along with Him? Remember that Romans 1:18-32 warns that God will judge those who think they do not need Him in their decision-making.

Be Friendly and Lovely

As the Scripture urges, if you have friends, you must endeavor first to show yourself as friendly as possible (Proverbs 18:24). You must be a true friend if you wish to make and keep real friends. Being friendly means behaving toward someone in a way that shows that you love them and are ready to listen to them, talk to them, and help them. A friend in need is a friend indeed, not only when there is a financial need but also in other aspects of life. You must be there for them always, whenever they need you. You must show love to them. Christ wants us to love and follow the path of peace with everyone. We must also pursue holiness because we cannot see the Lord without it.

Make yourself a Christ-like example; let your lifestyle preach the gospel of Christ without talking much. In friendship, actions speak louder than words. Ensure your communication is always graceful and seasoned with salt so your response will be uplifting, edifying, and pleasantly delivered. In the subsequent chapter, we will look at this topic in greater depth; you will discover that being friendly and lovely are significant factors in becoming a good leader. Remember, being a true friend to others will pave the way for excellence in your leadership.

07

PONDER POINTS

The person you chose to be in your
circle of friends today is one of the most
essential resolutions you will ever make
during your life journey.

Seven

CHOOSE THE RIGHT
FRIENDS NOW

> You may have the right aspirations, but you may never
> achieve your life goals until you pull the necessary trigger,
> especially regarding your relationships.

Blessed are those who refuse to walk in the counsel against
God's Holy Word. It is best to abstain from the way of sinners
and never sit in the seat of the scornful. God desires that we
not only delight in the law of the Lord but meditate on it
day and night. Following God's desire brings the blessings that
you desire. They shall be like the tree planted by the rivers
that bring forth their fruits in their season; their leaves shall
never wither, and whatsoever they do, they prosper (Psalms

1:1–3). The quintessential advantage to your future is that you can still choose and decide. Why not make the decision today? Your choices determine your destiny.

Even though some of us may believe in predestination, we can all agree that we are responsible for our actions. At one point in my life, I discovered that every successful person I have ever encountered had crossroads that dramatically changed their life for the better. That crossroad was when they made a clear, distinct, and determined unequivocal decision not to continue living the same way anymore. They took decisive action to achieve success. Some people make that decision in their teenage years, some in adulthood, some in old age, and most never make it at all.

Every great leap forward in your life comes after making a clear, distinct, and indubitable decision. Some people will decide for you if you cannot determine what is essential for your life. A wise person makes informed decisions; an ignorant fool follows public opinion. You may have the right aspirations, but you will achieve your life goals once you pull the necessary trigger, especially regarding your relationships. This is why a long time ago, I decided I would never continue a friendship or even a mere chat without relating it to the potential that propels and navigates my life.

Do you know that your destiny is not just fortuitous? It is God's design for you to choose from the choices placed before you. It would be best if you didn't always put yourself in the middle of the crossroad of life, as it poses too much danger for your life. It creates a high chance of getting slammed by upcoming traffic from both directions. In other words, stop playing the game, stop trying to be in the middle, and make that decision. With our discussions so far, will you decide to start selecting your friends by yourself? If you have decided, you have just set yourself on a path that leads to a more productive life. Your decisions determine your destiny. You are where you are today and may probably remain there for years to come simply because of the choices you have made. Deciding who to be with and who not to be with is one of those decisions you must make.

As someone once anonymously said, the average person does not know what to do with this life yet wants another one that will last forever. Please understand that it is not enough to decide; decisions, commitment, and patience mainly result in success. Can you recall this ponder point from chapter one? You will continue to be the same person and remain in the same place for years to come, except for these two most con-sequential things: your circle of friends and sources of infor-mation. Avoid negative people and their thought at all costs. These are the ones I fear so much because they are the greatest destroyers of self-confidence and self-esteem. The less you as-sociate with some of these people, the more you will improve your life. The wisdom book says that putting confidence in an unreliable person is like chewing with a sore tooth or trying to run with a broken foot (Proverbs 25:19).

Your true friends are those who bring out the best in you. You should be better, not worse after you've been around them. A few minutes of conversation with the right person can be more valuable than many years of study. So likewise, evil communication can be more destructive, as seen in the case of Eve and the serpent. If you look back to Adam and Eve's departure from the Garden of Eden, a land of abundance, it started with an evil communication with the serpent. Before you choose that friend, it will be paramount to investigate your options thoroughly. As the Book of Wisdom puts it, "The way that seems right to a person may be the way that leads to destruction" (Proverbs 14:12). The serpent may be a flake coming toward you, pretending to be friendly, like the one in the garden, but you may not notice it. Be wise in choosing your friends.

Don't always make decisions by the leading of your first impression. It may give you an inaccurate picture. You may want to ask, "Why should I be the one to choose my friends?" Some will say, "I am a free person," or "I meet different people daily, so everyone is my friend," or I am very social; everybody likes me," or "Nobody is my friend," and so on. You may even support your opinion with the Scriptures. We often say such things without considering our options and the characters and lifestyles involved. Is this because we are ignorant of who we are and the blessings and curses involved in friendship? We even go as far as describing people we don't know very well as friends. When I say people you don't know very well, I mean you have not gotten to know them to see if they are friendly enough to associate with them. You don't even know how much impact they can make in your life. Knowing if they are in positive alignment with the potentials that navigate your life is critical.

There is a great blessing for you when you find suitable companions. Again the psalmist agrees with this when he writes: The person who does not follow the path of sinners or sit in the companion of fools is divinely blessed. And if they delight in the Lord's word and meditate on it day and night, they shall be like a tree planted by the river. They shall yield fruit in and out of season, their leaf will never wither, and whatever they do flourishes (Psalms 1:1–3). It would help if you were wise in choosing the right friends now before it is too late and you end up in ruin. Though people may condemn you for being reserved and segregating yourself, it is worth it because of what you have inside of you and where God is taking or leading you. As children of God, we should always make sure we take the time to choose the right friends to please God because that is the primary condition of His blessings.

The great people we admire today chose their friends. In many cases, their friends were considered greater or more critical than they were at the initial stage of the journey, but before the middle of that voyage, they often became grander than their friends. That was only possible because they focused on their prospect and vision of the future. When you choose great friends, you will always thirst for greatness. The desire, passion, and drive for excellence will propel you to greatness.

NOTE:

Greatness is not just about finance or material things. Instead, greatness is about what you have inside of you and your ability and drive to be a solution to your generation. Greatness is about your influence and the positive differences you have made in the lives of others. The technology you enjoy today results from the kind of decisions made by the great men and women we admire today. Whenever you refuse to acknowledge the type of people that come into your life, you open uncontrollable access to your enemies, thus messing up your life. Understand this: if you choose the right friends now, you have not just decided your greatness but have taken a significant step.

People will always respect or disrespect you when they see your circle of friends. Remember that you are the world's light; you have no relationship with darkness or strange people. If you think you are a ray of sunshine, why not choose another ray of light so that you can both shine forth as a beam of light? Choose the Jesus kind of friends who are always concerned with how they can please God with their lives through service to God and humanity. With such friends, you can always edify each other with God's Word, pray together, and share ideas without fear or threat. These friends have goals, a drive for greatness, and exemplary character, and they acknowledge their purpose on earth. Sadly, you may be heading for doom if you refuse to choose the right friends now. Among the people you come across every day, you must make choices.

It's not enough to lay out your options; you must also

consider the probable result of each decision you make. Suppose the problem is an approaching enemy. In that case, considering the consequence of each alternative, like choosing the right friends and listing options, can be very helpful. For example, if selecting a particular friend means having to desert your family, harbor ungodly relationships, sin, disobedience, gossip, domestic violence, or sexual atrocities, choosing that particular friend could lead to many damaging habitual adaptations.

This damaging adaptation may lead to immoral behavior, failure, a lackadaisical attitude, behavioral disorder, wickedness, jail time, and a lousy record. All these may be significant reasons to choose another friend because that friend will destroy you. And don't forget to consider the spiritual impact your decisions will have on you, your vision, destiny, and those around you. On a more serious note, don't lose sight of how the friends you choose impact your relationship with God. Your relationships must always glorify God in all circumstances.

As a college student, I knew I was not academically strong because of my lackadaisical attitude and poor study habits. What helped me then was that I made friends with the best students in the class. I hung out with them until I became academically balanced, but I did not just leave them hanging; I also helped them achieve most things they couldn't have. You see, God used the friends I chose to deliver me from failure; today, I can continue to succeed wherever I find myself and no matter what I do. I always look for the person who knows better than I do so that I can gain from them. In other words,

I constantly endeavor to be in the circle of achievers. Before choosing someone as a friend, know that person properly. Just take your time and imagine the kind of people that person may be keeping as friends.

Think of great people like William Franklin "Billy" Graham Jr., an American Evangelical Christian ordained as a Southern Baptist minister. He rose to be in the limelight in 1949 and reached a core constituency of middle-class, moderately conservative Protestants. As of 2008, Graham's estimated lifetime audience, including radio and television broadcasts, topped 2.2 billion. William Henry "Bill" Gates III is a well-known American businessman, philanthropist, inventor, and computer programmer. Steven Paul "Steve" Jobs was an American entrepreneur, marketer, inventor, co-founder, chairman, and CEO of Apple Inc.

Warren Edward Buffett is a distinguished American businessman, investor, and humanitarian. He was the wealthiest investor of the twentieth century. He is presently the CEO, chairman, and leading shareholder of Berkshire Hathaway and ranked among the world's most affluent people repeatedly. He was the world's richest person in 2008. Buffett was also the third wealthiest in 2011 and 2012. *Time Magazine* named Buffett one of the world's most influential people and many other great men I may not mention here. Do you think these mentioned achievers would have friends who mess up their destiny or future? No, they probably all have great friends who were once higher or better than they were in one way or the other. The good thing about life is that if you are willing to learn what the most flourishing people did in any area and then do the same thing repeatedly, you will eventually get the same result. The greatness of a man is a product of his companions.

When you approach people, go by what is of interest to you. For example, if God calls you into ministry, look for more incredible people of like mind whom you can choose as friends. David and Jonathan demonstrated this in chapter 18 of 1 Samuel. My heartfelt prayer for you is that God will always furnish you with the wisdom to operate in life and that He will always guide your paths. The reality of life is that your love and passion for a particular activity, job, hobby, talent, gift, or game go a long way in choosing the right friend. Your love and devotion should attract those who mature in their thought and actions. When you make friends with great people or those who are like-minded in vision, you will often become significant with time.

You will see yourself sitting and dining with great people earlier than you could imagine. Keep away from negative people who will trivialize your ambition. Small people always do that; great people make you feel you can become great. You will be wide open to many areas of life and be connected to a network of great men, giving you access to places where even your possessions or money may never take you. Never underestimate yourself or feel overawed by intimidation when you seem to be the lowest in any circle of great people. If you follow this book well, you will discover that time is the difference between you and those great people. You may one day have to preside over their meetings. In other words, you may become a president in that robust network. There will be a point when people consider you better or more significant than they are. Those who consider you on the same level will seek to make you their mentor if only you can make that life-changing decision by choosing great people as your friends now.

Most times, when some great men and women discover that you are not harmful, have something to offer to the world, are ready to learn, and are drawing closer to them, they will bring you closer to them like a brother or a sister. And they will show you the way to greatness, but they only do this with loyal, hardworking, and honest people. Choosing those less than you may mean you only want to be disparaging. You cannot go to the top and stay firmly connected to the bottom of the ladder. They will create a severe drag on your flight. They will never allow you to soar to a greater height because some of them are comfortable at their current level. And they wouldn't want to be alone or lonely at the overcrowded bottom of life's ladder. There are still others who will keep you down while they get as much as possible from the little you have. They move on once they are content with all they can gain from you. Such people use you as their ladder to the top.

NOTE:

The way you choose your friends may be mistaken for pride or arrogance by some, but sometime in the future, they will realize they were wrong. You may be a role model or a mentor to some of them by then. I also encourage you to develop your self-worth. It is a strong feeling of confidence in yourself, the belief that you are great, and the knowledge that you are powerful. You are strengthened and empowered by Christ to do all things. Christ infuses me with His inner strength to ready me for anything that might come my way. This strength comes from understanding your identity in Christ (Philippians 4:13). The Bible tells us clearly how much God values you and how you should value yourself.

> I will continue to praise You because You have wonderfully and fearfully made me; Your works are marvelous in the sight of all. And this my soul acknowledges sincerely (Psalm 139:14). You are the salt of the earth: but if the salt has lost its savor, where will it be salted? It is then good for nothing but to be cast out and trampled under the foot of people. You are the light of the world. A city on a hill cannot be hidden (Matthew 5:13–14).

For as many as the Spirit of God leads, they are known and function as God's son. God has not given us the Spirit of bondage again to be fearful; instead, He gave us the Spirit of adoption. For this reason, each day we cry, Abba, Father. The Spirit bears witness to our spirit, which makes us know that we are God's children. And if we are children, then we are heirs, God's heirs, and joint heirs with Christ. And if it is true that we suffer with Christ, then we may also be glorified together with Him (Romans 8:14–17). Your identity is in Christ as much as Christ is in you. I hope you understand this now so you will know the right decision to make when choosing that friend. By now, you should have started to consider and have perhaps discovered whether the friends you are keeping right now are worth it. It would be best if you also discovered whether they fit into the path of your destiny.

I plead with you today that you choose the right friends wisely. It is better to do it now and bear all the pain and insult now rather than feel sorry when it is too late. When choosing your friends, ensure they don't influence you with worldly things like money, material things, or fleshy desires. If you allow them to blow you away with worldly things, you will create enmity with God. Don't you know that the world's friendship is tantamount to making God your enemy? It is straightforward; if you make friends with the world, you have at the same time declared enmity with God (James 4:4), so be wise. Don't start making friends just because of their wealth and the little enjoyment that may later bring about a life of poverty or suffering. Please don't allow so-called friends to in-fluence you with material things; you may not know when you will cheaply sell your birthright, as Esau sold his to Jacob.

Choose the Company of Eagles Now and Soar to Greater Heights in Life

Before you decide, do you know that love shows a man's character? A genuine nature of a man is revealed by what he loves dearly. As a person thinks in their heart, so is the person according to their heart's content. Also, as one loves, so is the person according to their passion, so you may confidently designate the person. If the person is a lover of honor, we can designate that person to be ambitious. If one is a lover of pleasure, one can identify them as sensual; if one primarily loves the world, we can say they are greedy. If one loves righteousness, they may be religious; if they love Christ and the things above with preeminent love, they are heavenly-minded, sincere, and faithful men or women of God.

Be selective about your external influences because your brain is multidimensional. Our external influence and how we respond to them influence us internally. Almost everything you see, hear, read, smell, touch, feel, or say if not under control, can easily influence you. You have a mission in life that needs to be accomplished. And it is mission-critical for you to get with the right people. Associate with positive, goal-oriented individuals who promote and inspire you, as that is the way that leads to greatness. Know from now on that you are fully responsible for everything in your life, and you will someday have to give a complete account of it.

08

PONDER POINTS

Sharing, caring, daring, and loving are
the four essential things that always lead
to a more celebrated life.

Eight

FOUR ELEMENTS OF A RELATIONSHIP THAT MAKES ONE A TRUE FRIEND

> It is by loving instead of being loved (as it is more blessed to give than to receive) that one can get closer to the soul of another.

I cannot talk about friendship without helping you become a true friend to others. You cannot be a true friend to others without being friendly and lovely. As the Book of Wisdom clarifies, "a man with friends must show himself friendly; there is a friend that sticks closer than a brother" (Proverbs 18:24). Friendliness means behaving toward someone in a way that evinces your love for them. It also indicates that you want to talk to them and are always ready to listen. To be referred to as a true friend, you should always be friendly and lovely. Love and friendliness do not mean you should be perfect; only God is perfect. At the end of this chapter, you will discover that being a true friend makes you a good leader. When you are friendly and lovely, you can lead in any circle you find your-self in because you have the primary characteristics of a good leader. Let's examine the four elements of a true friend and a good leader.

Love People

In His commandment, Christ expects you to love one another as He has loved you. Christ also made us understand that someone who says they love God and hate their brothers or sisters is a liar. For if the person loves not their brothers or sisters, whom they have seen, how can they love God, whom they have not seen (1 John 4:20)? If God so loved us, we ought also to love one another (1 John 4:11–21). Love is an act of unconditional forgiveness, a tenderhearted way of life that becomes a habit. It is by loving instead of being loved (as it is more blessed to give than to receive) that one can come closer to the soul of another. Being loved is the second-most preeminent thing in the world; loving someone is preeminent. Love sought after is good, but love established unsought is healthy. You must love them for you to be the right friend.

Love people for who they are (their personality), not their color, race, or culture. Do you know that our willingness to open up about who we are encourages trust and openheartedness from the other person? So be yourself and be genuine when showing love to people. Love is not a once-in-a-while business. It is the continuous, decisive action to live as God has commanded. As I said earlier, love should be a way of life. We must do everything in love. It is factual that when we act in love, we can live reliably, sensitively, ruggedly, and tenderheartedly in all relationships and our day-to-day lives.

Sincere love and submission to Christ provide an indubitable power for us to love and effectuate all things. The Scriptures have assured us that we can do everything through Christ, who strengthens us. In today's world, nobody cares how much you know until they see how much you care. God made this clear and comprehensible to us when he said, "And you shall love the Lord thy God with all thy heart, soul, and all thy might and strength. This is the first commandment, and the second is like this: thou shall love thy neighbors as thyself. No other commandment is greater than these" (Mark 12:30–31).

From the word of God (logos), as you have read, love is the greatest commandment in life. You must love people without reservation to please God, just as you have loved yourself. In the book of John, Christ maintains the new commandment He gave us, that you love one another as He has loved you.

All men know that you are disciples by this if you treat one another with love (John 13:34–45). When you show love to people, it preaches the gospel of Christ; as they say, "actions speak louder than words." To prove your identity in Christ, you must love others as you love yourself.

I can hear you asking yourself, where do I start? Don't stress it. We learn to walk by walking, run by running, fly by flying, work by working, and in the same manner, we learn to love people by loving. The journey of a thousand miles always starts with the first mile, so start loving from this moment and make it a habit.

Apostle Paul greatly emphasized the essence of love; he wrote this letter in 1 Corinthians 13 to correct the deceptive notions in the Corinthian church at that time. He wrote about the excellence and beauty of love in his writings. I love how Apostle Paul made it so straightforward and understandable that even a little kid will understand the merit of love. If one articulates with the tongues of men and angels but has no love for others, one will become a noisy and annoying distraction. And if anyone is gifted to prophesy and delivers new messages from God to His people, is knowledgeable, and understands all mysteries, that person is nothing without love.

In the same way, if you have sufficient faith to move mountains but lack the love to reach out to others, it isn't beneficial. It is nonsense if you give all your possessions to feed people experiencing poverty and willfully surrender your body as a sacrifice but have no love. Love endures with patience and serenity. Love is kind and thoughtful. Love is never envious.

Love does not brag and is not arrogant. It is not rude. It is not self-seeking. One cannot easily provoke love, nor is it overly sensitive. Love does not consider a wrong endured. Love dislikes injustice, prejudice, and stereotypes but rejoices when the truth prevails.

Love bears all things regardless of the outcome. Love constantly looks for the best in each one. Prophecies will pass away, tongues will cease, and the gift of special knowledge will pass away, but love remains steadfast during difficult times without weakening. Love never fails. There is a kind of faith that abides and trusts in God and all His promises. Then there is hope that is confidently pregnant of eternal salvation. And there is also the unselfish love for others that grows out of God's love. As for these three, the greatest of these is love (1 Corinthians 13). Now, with all you have read so far, how can you be a true friend without loving? It is scripturally and practically impossible.

Listen to Them

You must all be quick to listen, Brother James urges (James 1:19). Listening is the potential to accumulate and precisely elucidate messages in the communication process. It is central to adequate communication. With this potential, one could easily understand the communication between two or more people. With the element of listening in communication, the conveyor of the message may become more satisfied over time. This satisfaction comes from being heard by your specific audience. Excellent listening skills can lead to better satisfaction in communication and increased productivity. They can also lead to longevity with fewer relationship mistakes and increased information sharing for a healthier and happy friendship. Most prosperous leaders and entrepreneurs ascribe their success to sensitive and efficient listening ability. This technique supports all honest, healthy, and lasting friendships. It is worthwhile to develop your listening ability because it is the building block of a happy lifestyle.

Active-listening skills also benefit us in various parts of our personal lives. Most of our friends have improved self-worth and self-assurance, academic work excellence, or health and well-being due to effective listening. Listening is quite different from hearing. Hearing alludes to the sounds you hear while listening entails more than that: it demands focus. It means paying attention to details, not only the tale but also how they express their message with body gestures, language, and voice. It is also being aware of both verbal and nonverbal messages.

Your listening ability depends on how you discern and comprehend these messages. The most fundamental and efficient way to connect with others is to listen. All they may ever need from you is to be quiet and listen, as this is one of the most valuable things we can freely give each other. Sensitive listening demands more concentration and proper use of other senses, not just hearing the spoken words alone. In other words, hearing is different from listening.

You must involve more than just your ears to listen sensitively and efficiently. An effective listener will listen to what a friend communicates verbally and what is left unvoiced. Effective listening involves observing body language and discerning inconsistencies and self-contradiction between verbal and nonverbal messages. For instance, if a friend tells you they are happy with everything while tears run down their cheek and they have negative facial expressions, the verbal and nonverbal messages are in dissension. Your friend may not mean what they say or are just trying to be positive.

Sensitive listening and hearing are open gold mines to friendship. In reality, we have yet to utilize the art of listening before we talk. It lolls within us like a shipload of unmined treasure. It is good that we understand that every one of us has barriers that impede our listening to someone. Some may be simple, and others may be complex, but remember that one way to show that you love them is by communicating acceptance.

We often find ourselves doing more talking and less listening. At the end of the conversation, we recommend a solution without being patient enough to listen to what the person is trying to relate to us. These always result in arguments and frustration. Patiently listening to friends in love is one way of expressing such acceptance. An example, in this case, is the life of Jesus Christ, our perfect friend, who is the author and the finisher of our faith. He is always expeditious in listening to us, whether we are right or wrong. Care and affection can often be evidenced by how much we listen to people.

Listening is a creative force, and it is highly magnetic in nature. Several scientific observations have expressed that the friends who listen to us are the friends we are inclined to; we are inclined to dwell within the radius of such friends. When we are listened to, it recreates our mindset and gives fresh vitality to our faith in a possible solution. It makes us unfold and expand in various aspects of life.

You may ask, What will I say after listening? Remember that Christ is in you, and you are in Christ. Christ in you is the hope of glory (Colossians 1:27). The Holy Spirit will always guide you in what to say in every situation that comes to your attention. When people discover that you are an active listener, they will always want to be around you. Active listening means you will listen to them sensitively and efficiently with love. This kind of listening does not go without passion, empathy, and the willingness to help.

Talk to Them

Let the word of Christ dwell in you richly in all wisdom, teaching, and admonishing one another in Psalms, hymns, and spiritual songs, singing with grace in your heart for the Lord (Colossians 3:16). We must be affluent in God's Word and wisdom to talk to friends in a Godly manner. To win and keep good friends, you must learn to speak regarding the other person's regard. The essential point you need to remember is this: to be of real help to your friends as they grapple with the issues of life, you must try and think of yourself in their situations, encouraging, sympathizing, and empathizing with them.

It is not helpful to espouse a "take it or leave it" attitude.

You may have to spend lots of time trying to explicate issues that are obvious to you but which your friends seem to have enormous difficulty grasping. Always rely on God to help you whenever you find yourself in this kind of situation. You will also have to create time for them because it takes time to communicate, work through conflicts, and build healthy relationships.

In friendship, James warns us never to slander, defame or judge one another (James 4:11). We are never supposed to speak words that tear down our friends. Scriptures oblige us to speak morally and spiritually, elevating words. We should say words that inspire happiness and encouragement and cause positive changes in the life of our friends. "Let your speech at all times be gracious, seasoned with salt, so that you may know how to answer anyone who demands your response" (Colossians 4:6).

True friendship is a dedication to love, a fitting into each other, an apprehension of caring, sharing, and sacrificing. It is out of that dedication that action must follow, so talk about your friend's situation today. I will encourage you never to criticize, condemn, gossip, backbite, or diminish people. If you do so to those you are to love, help, and service, then you've yet to learn about the teaching or revelation of Christ. You must ask for God's wisdom daily and have a fear of God in you because the fear of the Lord is the beginning of wisdom: and the knowledge of the Holy Spirit is understanding (Proverbs 9:10).

Always study God's Word so that words that come out of your mouth can have the power to influence someone to align themself with the will of God. And you cannot have this unless you subject yourself to God's Word. You cannot give what you don't have. Out of the good treasure of one's heart, a good person's heart brings forth that which is good. And out of the evil treasure of one's heart, an evil person brings forth that which is evil. For of the abundance of one's heart one's mouth speaks (Luke 6:45). So, now we know that it is out of the abundance of the word of God in your heart that your mouth will speak out to people.

The word of God in you is powerful, but you may not know its power until you talk it out. The word of God is living, active, and powerful. This power makes it operative, energizing, and effective. It is sharper than any two-edged sword. It penetrates the division of our soul and spirit and the deepest parts of our human nature. The word of God has the unlimited power to expose and judge our hearts' very thoughts and intentions. And not a creature concealed from His sight exists, but all things are open and exposed and revealed to the eyes of Him with whom we must give account (Hebrews 4:12).

Going by the above Scripture, we can see that when the word of God is entirely in you, you can discern another man's thoughts and the intent of his heart. It is paramount to know that you can only consistently keep people's attention by focusing on what they value and the issues that threaten their happiness. You may want to ask again, How can you know that? The actual answer is that except the Lord builds your house, you may be building it in vain. All your sweat may be for nothing. The guards will watch in vain, except the

Lord watches over a city. So likewise, except the Lord speaks through you, your wise counsel may become foolishness to the hearer. Lastly, always explain to them clearly because exhortation without clarification will undoubtedly lead to frustration. As I have stressed in this book, be gracious in using your words. The goal is to bring out the best in others, especially when conversing with them. Your conversation with them should be uplifting, not putting them down and never cutting them out.

Help Them

Friendship deals with one's feelings and thoughts out of a desire to be familiar with another's inner life—and to care, dare, and share one's burden. It is more impressive to love others more than they will ever ask of you. God desires you to be your brother's or sister's keeper, bearing one another's burden in love. I've discovered that prosperous people always have the quest for opportunities to help others.

In contrast, vain people always ask, What will be my gain? Life's most untiring and dire questions are "What are you doing for others?" "What are your contributions toward helping others?" and "What is your impact on this generation?" To be celebrated, you must help others to the top, consulting their weaknesses, relieving them of complaints, and striving to uplift them. In doing so, you will most efficaciously boost yourself. A friend in need may be a friend indeed. They need your help as a friend. You should be concerned about them just as you are concerned about yourself.

Treat them as you would treat God if God were physically with you. You can also help them by forgiving them if they offended you because Christ said we should forgive. Lead them to Christ and introduce eternal life to them. Please make sure you are interested in their spiritual and physical well-being. Help them with resources that will improve their lives. Don't be selfish to your friends; leave sentiment out of your daily dealings with people. Pray for your friends; your breakthrough may depend on it. Remember that the Lord turned the captivity of Job when he prayed for his friends.

God is always happy anytime you pray for your friends; you cannot pray for your friends and remain the same. You will always have enough people to celebrate you all your life, but only if you help enough other people to be honored. Remember the ponder points; these four essential things lead to a more illustrious life: sharing, caring, daring, and most of all, loving always. Assign yourself the purpose of making others happy and fruitful. Your friends have a way of becoming what you encourage them to be.

If you are sharp-eyed at what happens around you, it will be easy to decipher the two types of people in the world: those who live for themselves and those who live to help others. The first group is the vain people, while the second group is the flourishing ones. It pays to invest in others and help others because your life depends on it; it pays high dividends. Apostle Paul encouraged us to continue to do good unto all people as we have the opportunity, especially those of the community of faith (Galatians 6:10).

In doing all these, you make yourself an excellent leader among your friends and beyond, as these are the fundamental qualities of a good leader. Good leaders love their people, listen to their people, talk to their people, and help them as much as they can. These premises prove that if you are worthy of being called a true friend, you are also worthy of being a leader. No wonder Jesus Christ is the perfect friend and the most famous excellent, righteous, and inspiring leader. We will dwell more on this ideal friend in the tenth chapter.

09

PONDER POINTS

Therefore, as God's chosen people, holy
and dearly loved, clothe yourselves with
compassion, kindness, humility, gentleness,
and patience. Bear with each other and
forgive one another if any of you has a
grievance against someone.

Forgive as the Lord forgave you.
(Colossians 3:12-13 NIV)

Nine

TIPS FOR BECOMING
A BETTER FRIEND

> Make allowance for each other's faults, and forgive
> anyone who offends you. Remember, the Lord forgave
> you, so you must forgive others. Above all, clothe your-
> selves with love, which binds us all together in perfect
> harmony (Colossians 3:13-14 NIV).

Let Love and Tolerance Be Your Way of Life

You can show tolerance by respecting, accepting, and appreciating the rich diversity of our world's cultures, customs, and
traditions. You could also show your respect for others' modes
of articulation and ways of representing our uniquely human
nature. Tolerance can also be viewed as a way of expressing

thoughts and feelings. Still, most significantly, it is an action that gives us inner peace in our various distinctions. It gives reverence to those different from us. It is also the wisdom to recognize human values and the courage to act upon them graciously.

Tolerance is simply the willingness to tolerate even in disparity. We are all from different demographics, settings, environments, and cultures, as you know pretty well. I know fully well that it is not that easy to understand someone who is not from the same background. Loving and tolerating people, regardless of where they come from or how they are made up, allows you to develop good relationships with people others would never consider. Just imagine how lovely and welcoming this world will be if we let love and tolerance be our guide.

Avoid Discriminating, Stereotyping, and Prejudice

Do not judge others so that you will not be judged likewise. You will be treated as you treat others. The standard you use in judging is the standard by which you will also be judged (Matthew 7:1–2). Discrimination is a behavior that unjustly treats people. It is prejudicial treatment given to different categories of individuals or things unequally because of their group, memberships, or similarities. Most discriminatory behaviors often begin with negative stereotypes and prejudices.

A stereotype is an extensively held but firm, false, and oversimplified image or idea of a particular type of people, place, or thing. A mistaken belief distorts the truth about a specific individual or group. This generalization allows for little or no individual differences or physical, social, and spiritual variation. It can be positive or negative, but in most cases, it is damaging. It is based chiefly on images projected by mass media or characters passed on by parents, friends, and other members of society.

Prejudice is a preconceived opinion, judgment, attitude, or idea about a group or its members that is not based on genuine reason. Prejudice is not always negative, but in our usage, we deal with the negative attitude in this book. It usually co-occurs with ignorance, fear, or hatred. It is mainly initiated by a complex psychological process that starts with attachment to a cohort of acquaintances or a circle of family and friends. In most cases, prejudice is always aimed at outgroups or minorities.

Our world is heterogeneous; you must understand that the people you deal with daily are diverse in their hearts' content, character, attitude, and thought processes. If you are sharp-eyed or sharp-minded enough, you must have discovered that the other people in your life—family members, fellow students, colleagues, and neighbors—are different from you. It may be in height, symmetry, weight, physique, body, skin or hair color, mode of dressing, financial status, and language. Some may sound unlike us in their native dialect, accent, articulation, tone, vocal clarity, and voice inflection. And some may be disparate in intellect, earning potential, athleticism, education, politics, social philosophies, sexual orientations, religion, beliefs, birth, brainpower, etc. For you to enjoy a happy and healthy relationship with people, these essential differences should be well respected as they will help us get along well.

It is pretty hapless that many of us were taught to judge others unlike us with uncomplimentary remarks. For many of us, it all started when our parents or guardians protected us by saying, "Don't trust or talk to strangers." During grade school, some of us were told to "care for the homeless" but never walk near them because they can hurt, infect, or kill you. And maybe finally, by high school age, everything we've been taught by our parents, guardians, and others we trusted comes together to form our thought process.

Our observation of real life, in movies, television, mass media, and things we've experienced directly and indirectly through others' behavior helped transmute this negative way of life into prejudices. So almost without realizing it, we have learned to stereotype an entire population based on the attitude and beliefs of just a few. Unfortunately, we built some prejudices on a solid foundation of falsehood and fear of the unknown.

However, it has been seen that stereotyping, in most cases, damages those who are stereotyped. It can also harm those who believe the stereotype cannot affect them. When you think it cannot affect you, you will do nothing to stop it; you will tolerate the acts that foster stereotypes. As you strive daily for happy and healthy relationships, you must forsake your prejudice, stereotype, and discrimination in your daily activities with people. Your potential to become a better friend increases tremendously as you open your mind to the many differences you encounter. This openness of mind will also help you learn how these differences can enhance your relational capacity and other people's quality of life.

Rehearse Friendly Greetings

It always feels good to give an excellent first impression. For this reason alone, you may need to sometimes stand in front of your mirror and rehearse your first smile and greeting. It would be best to let others recognize that you care and want to learn more about them. For starters and those who are shy, try and work this out so that it may become real and a little easier for you.

Try Reaching Out to Others

If you wait for others to reach out to you for a relationship or friendship, you may be waiting a long time. We live in the days when people are unwilling or maybe scared to reach out in friendship. It is critical to know that most of them may have experienced painful relationships and may not be in a hurry to get back into a relationship, making them susceptible to others. If you are going to have a relationship with someone, realize that you may have to be the one to initiate the relationship, as this may help you select and choose your friends.

Get Out There and Meet People

Sitting at home like a loner or isolating yourself will not put you in a position to get that friend of your choice. Join a club, fellowship with people, volunteer in your church, school, or community, and participate in activities that physically involve other people. Sometimes it's good to take slow walks to enable you to stop and talk to others. I encourage you to get out there and meet people.

Have More Than One Friend

Most healthy and happy people have many connections, a few good friends, and two or three very close associates. It is precarious to have just one close friend. Having all your eggs in one basket or putting them on only one friend is herculean. No person should ever think of meeting those demands because no person can carry all the necessary virtues. Remember, as we are all unique, everybody has something special to offer. It is inevitable that when you have more than one good friend, you will live a healthier life and make a better friend, as two good heads are better than one.

Never Quit; Go the Second Mile

You will never have good friends if you quit a friendship or relationship at first disappointment. Remember, winners never quit, and quitters never win. Those you love most in life disappoint you more than anyone else. Always allow love and grace to operate in your relationship.

There Should Be Common Interests

Don't waste time accommodating the things that detach you from others. Find consensus. Always look for something meaningful to get you communicating. Remember what I said earlier: a long time ago, I decided I would never continue a friendship or even a mere chat without relating it to the potential that propels and navigates my life.

Give Recognition and Encouragement

Most people attach so much value to recognition. We all need someone to lift us at various points in life. Always recognize others' achievements and tell them their importance to you. This will enhance them with the opportunity for self-satisfaction and good feeling. It is paramount to know that it is not what you say to people but how you make them feel that is momentous.

Be Flexible

They may dress differently from you or not want to eat in the same restaurants. Be flexible. You only love eating in fast food joints, and your friends like eating the food they prepared themselves; one of you will have to be flexible if you will enjoy your relationship. The perfect example of someone who is a master of maintaining and creating perfect friendships is Jesus Christ. You will make an excellent friendship if you follow Christ's example. Be flexible in any relationship you find yourself in. Being too rigid stunts the growth of any relationship. Be flexible and enjoy your relationship.

Let Truth and Honesty Be Your Core Values

Honesty may seem like a slippery slope; it is practically more challenging than it sounds. A weak friendship may not survive the test of truth and honesty. It must be the foundation of any relationship. Any friendship that is not based on reality will not last long. Any form of ingenuity in your relationship will eventually bring the relationship to an end. That you are honest does not mean that you should be unkind, blunt, or disrespectful. It just means that you should lovingly share the truth. I will advise you to be gentle because how you present the truth may turn the other person off. Truth and honesty may hurt sometimes, but only true friendship can survive and grow. Let truth and honesty be the value of your relationships.

Learn to Be Reticent but Supportive

It is not uncommon to have a friend grappling in her marriage at some point or having difficulty with family members or another close friend. This may be the time for you to be reserved because this relationship issue will often be resolved. So, if you say nasty things about your friend's spouse, family members, or friends when they are at loggerheads, they will not be happily recollected by them. You may not be liked if that happens. You may be misunderstood. Even if you feel like buttressing any of them, be quiet for a while. All you may need to do is listen and care for them as you can. Caring for them does not mean you start quoting all the related scriptural verses you can remember. It does not mean you should compare and contrast their problem with past experience. Caring should be done empathetically. In most cases, caring may also be for you to listen attentively.

Understand this, my dear brothers and sisters: you must all be quick to listen, slow to speak, and delayed to get angry (James 1:19). For example, she may try to get you to belabor her husband or family members verbally. Please, for God's sake, don't fall for it, but always make sure you are encouraging and supportive. If it is a case of an abusive relationship or a threat to life, then some of these rules may not apply, but let wisdom guide you always.

Abscond from All Appearances of Gossip and Backbiting

In my experience, I have gotten close to people who talk, tear down, destroy, and rundown other people in their absence. Shortly after, I realized that if they can tear other people down behind them to me, it's plain and straightforward—the same can be done to me. Avoid the mistake of believing that you are exempted from any form of gossip and backbiting; the same will be done to you. You may not necessarily need to talk about the scandal, but by laughing and listening, you give your participation, and in so doing, you encourage the act.

Never luxuriate in any form so you won't fret about your malicious talk being thrown back at you. This will help avoid the endless circle of regretting and apologizing for everything you have said. I understand that we occasionally struggle in our relationships with others, but it is not a valid reason to tear someone down behind closed doors. Imagine a situation where you've verbally destroyed somebody who regrettably became your friend. If you've ever indulged in this kind of action before getting close to that person, they will find out someday and may likely be hurt.

Don't Be Too Sensitive

When you are excessively sensitive, you will overthink yourself and your feelings about how everything goes in your relationship. If your close friends must be cautious when they are in your radius and constantly fret about hurting your feelings, the friendship will experience stunted growth. As I said, a sincere and lasting friendship requires honesty. It will be impracticable to be honest with you if you are overly sensitive. At times in our life, close friends amazingly address us in an unpleasant, irksome, and vexatious manner. If you ever happen to find yourself in a situation like this, all you need to do is to recall that the Scriptures warn us to be slow to anger. This means you should always try to give yourself time to think about it before you speak.

Make necessary and favorable considerations before reacting to avoid regrettable actions. If your feelings remain hurt, you should first calm yourself down and then discuss it, explaining why it hurt so badly. If that friend is a true friend, that may help clarify, correct, and build your friendship further. You don't have to fear misunderstanding them sometimes. You also don't have to live with the fear of making mistakes because it can help you better understand each other. Know today that if you are too sensitive in any relationship, you will never get the best out of that relationship.

Don't Get Yourself in the Middle

Friendship has its daily struggles, ups, and downs. Sometimes some relationships may break, and if you are not careful, you could end up in the middle. As I said earlier, be reserved but supportive. It would help to keep yourself from coming in between friends, marriages, families, and associates. Always encourage them to work it out on their own. The danger of getting yourself in the middle is awful. This is because, toward the end, they may both turn against you. So, it is wise to stop being nosy. Get out of other people's matters, mainly when it doesn't concern you. Scriptures warned that a perverse person sows discord, and those who whisper separates close friends (Proverbs 16:28). You do not want to be described as such.

Be Sacrificial

Occasionally, actual friendship demands giving up some of your desires. For example, if a friend gets married, gives birth, or gets a new demanding job, this may mean that you may get less time with them than you habitually had before the marriage, baby, or career. Know that this may not necessarily mean your time with that friend is not of the same quality as you are used to; it is just a difference in quantity. To maintain a healthy relationship, you must make unexpected sacrifices as a true friend. Rather than feeling downhearted, try to be understanding and gracious, with the understanding that it could be you instead. Life is full of changes, stages, and phases that are ineluctable. True friendship can adapt to circumstances and grow through it all. If your friendship is not genuine, you will find that relationship to be temporal during the test and trial of different times and weather.

Don't Be Quick to Make Assumptions

Friends may get busy sometimes, which may even dispossess them of the time to call, chat, or maybe stay on the phone for a long conversation. We should be mindful of these and understand carefully as situations demand. It is paramount always to let close friends know how busy your schedule may be. This is so that they don't quickly get aggrieved if you cannot make that call or engage them in a normal lengthy conversation at that particular time. There is this assumption that frequently befalls us in friendships. It is when we try to engage in a vital discussion without fully acknowledging the person's state of mind or situation.

In most cases, assumptions get us in serious trouble and always squash relationships. Please don't always believe what other people say about your friends without making an unbiased inquiry. Those who spread rumors about other people may do so because they envy their healthy and happy relationship. Learn to eschew and pay no attention to them, as they may be your haters, and haters don't always deserve your attention. The only attention they need is the one of Christ to change them. Beloved, if you desire to be a better friend than you are right now, make these tips your guide and watch your relationships blossom. Like any other relationship, making a true friendship work takes lots of time and effort. The benefit is that the reward is worth the work.

10

PONDER POINTS

One exciting and fascinating thing
about God's love is that you can never
get enough of it, and you can do nothing
to make it more or less.
His love is unequaled, indubitable,
and unambiguous.

Ten

THE PERFECT FRIEND

> **No one has shown stronger love and affection than Christ who laid down His life for His friends and haters.**

His name is Jesus. Let me tell you more about Him; I have long been waiting for this. There was a time when Jesus went on a journey with His disciples to the villages of Caesarea Philippi, and on their way, Jesus asked His disciples, "Whom do men say I am?" At this point, He wanted them to tell Him who they thought He was. He wanted to know how they see Him and think of Him. And they answered Him and said, "Some call you John the Baptist, some others Elijah, and some believe you are one of the prophets." Then He turned to His disciple and asked them, "But whom do you say I am?" This time He wanted to know directly what the disciples called Him or what they thought of Him. Then Peter replied, "You are Christ the Messiah, the anointed One."

I can't even envision Jesus asking me that same question to-day; I will call him the author and the finisher of my faith, the bright and morning star, the omnipotent, omnipresent, and omniscient God. The advocate, the lamb of God, the bread of life, the rose of Sharon, my mind regulator, the Holy One, the head of my family. I can go on and on; He is the All-Sufficient God.

The name Jesus in New Testament Greek is *Iesosus* (e-ay-sees). You can find the origin of that name in the Old Testament name Joshua, Jehoshuah, or Jehoshaua, pronounced "Jehohushawa" (ye-ho-shoo-ah) or "Yehow shua." His name was not based on random choice or personal whim of any fashion but on His primary mission in life. And His mission was de-termined and concluded from the foundation of the world. Christ was to save us from our sins (Revelation 13:8) with one sacrifice that would last forever.

The importance of the name of Jesus does not end with His noble mission in life. His actions and way of life project Him as the only savior of humanity. He was the only perfect friend who stretched out the heavens alone and spread the earth by himself (Isaiah 44:24). He came to earth to save us all. God did not send someone else to save the world. He came Himself. In Jesus Christ, we find the most extraordinary profundity of love, the ever-green portion of joy, and the copious measure of peace. He is the initiator of love. The Scripture states: "Greater love has no man than this that a man lay down His life for His friends" (John 15:13).

His love is permanent, wholehearted, unswerving, eager, and genuine. His love never fails. He is that special friend always with you, in and for you (Emmanuel). You can see that Jesus Christ is the only friend who can always be there for you. As He said in the Bible, "And lo I am with you always, even to the world's end." (Mathew 28:20). He is the omnipotent God, the omniscient God, and the omnipresent God. No one has shown stronger love and affection than Christ, who laid down his life for his friends. His love continues the same yesterday, today, and always, even in the absence of your love.

He has always loved you, no matter the height of your sins. He is the ever-loving God. He reaches out to people from every walk of life to attain a personal relationship with them. He does not care if they are rich or poor because His love is equitable. From the Scriptures, He even reached out to a Samaritan woman whom others never liked, and they ridiculed him for having such a relationship. Your status in life is not a concern and will never be.

If we understand that Christ has our love, we can see He has our all. Until we admit that He has our love, Christ will never have what He deserves from us. True love holds back nothing from Christ when it is sincerely set upon him. If we sincerely love Christ, He will have our time. He will be at our services, and He will also have the use of all our resources. He will also have our compassion, freedom, and all whenever He demands them.

In the same way, when God loves any of us, he will never withhold anything good and beautiful from us. Remember, God did not keep his only begotten Son from dying for our sins. Just like the Scripture said, "He that spared not his own Son, but delivered Him up for us all, how shall he not with him also freely give us all things" (Romans 8:32)? Christ loves us. He gives us everything we need: his preeminence to justify us in all areas of life, his Spirit to consecrate us, his grace to adorn us, and His glory, our royal diadem. From the moment we confess that we love Christ sincerely, it is demanded that we lay the whole thing down at His feet and give up everything at His command and services. You must also give up your old ways, pick up your cross daily, and faithfully follow Him daily for the rest of your lives.

New Friend, Meet Jesus Christ, the Ever-Perfect Friend

It is evident that Christ already knows all about you. When I say all about you, I mean your past, present, and beautiful future. He is the beginning and the end. He designed and created you. He saw both the fortunate and unfortunate things you have gone through in life. Christ has been waiting patiently, with all eagerness all this time, just for you to reach the point where you want a wonderful fellowship restored between you and God the Father. A relationship that concurs with God's original plan. This will only come about when the Holy Spirit finds His way into your heart. He intends to make your heart his home since your body is supposed to be a temple of God.

Before I move on, I would like to clarify a few fundamental facts about Jesus Christ and His place in the Trinity. This is so we don't end up bewildering ourselves with the names, titles, and terms used. For the sake of those new to this, God, as it was illuminated in the Holy Scriptures, is a Spirit. He is the All-Mighty God. He is the creator of the universe, including all the living and non-living creatures, the stars, planets, humans, and everything that's not artificial. God has always been. God is the beginning and the end and has been before the beginning of creation. We have always seen and experienced God in three distinct personalities.

He is God the Father, the fountainhead of all life. Christ is the Son of God, who came to reenact the relationship we lost through Adam in the Garden of Eden. He came to bridge the gap between the Father and us. His blood was shed on the cross of Calvary that made us pure, holy, and acceptable before the Father. That is why we have perfect access to speak directly to the Father. The Holy Spirit, the third person of the Trinity, is the comforter. He comes into our lives after we accept Christ as our Lord and Savior. His principal duty is to guide, remind, teach, and comfort us. His duty in our life depends on the situation and our availability.

It is understandable if you are new to this; it has never been an easy endeavor to comprehend the Trinity of God. He has and will always make His Son the center of attention. He wants us to converge all our interests and activities on His

Son. He desires that we elevate Him more than any person or thing so that all men would venerate him. It is fascinating to know that understanding that aspect of God helps us appreciate the other part of God. This understanding helps a lot even though we get our terms mixed up most times while learning about God.

He will be glorified and will also glorify Himself in us if we can focus our hearts and sight on His begotten Son, the author and the finisher of our faith. He will be glorified if we can believe and obey all His spoken and written words (Rhema and Logos). For this reason, even a little child, regardless of age, can learn to love Jesus and grow in wisdom, knowledge, and a clearer understanding of their faith.

It's so human of us to have believed that we have outgrown the need for Jesus when we make new friends. It's imperative to know that God desires to be friends with us far more than we do with Him. For this reason alone, He sent His only begotten Son to close the gap between the Father and us. It is wholly spiritual and invisible, but it affects our lives physically, emotionally, and positively. I am living proof of that. I will wrap this up with an old song that dearly ministers to me. I believe this life-touching hymn will bless your soul. It may help affix your mind onto Jesus. You may not know the song, but it is effortless to find on the internet. It is "**What a Friend we have in Jesus**," written by Joseph M. Scriven (1855).

WHAT A FRIEND WE HAVE IN JESUS

What a friend we have in Jesus, all our sins and griefs to bear!

What a privilege to carry, everything to God in prayer!

O, what peace we often forfeit, O, what needless pain we bear,

All because we do not carry, everything to God in prayer.

Have we trials and temptations? Is there trouble anywhere?

We should never be discouraged; Take it to the Lord in prayer.

Can we find a friend so faithful? Whom will all our sorrows share?

Jesus knows our every weakness; Take it to the Lord in prayer.

Are we weak and heavy-laden? Cumbered with a load of care,

Precious Savior, still our refuge. Take it to the Lord in prayer.

Do thy friends despise, forsake thee? Take it to the Lord in prayer!

In his arms, he'll take and shield thee, thou wilt finds solace there.

Blessed Savior, Thou hast promised, Thou wilt all our burdens bear.

May we ever, Lord, be bringing all to Thee in earnest prayer.

Soon in glory, bright unclouded, there will be no need for prayer.

Rapture, praise, and endless worship will be our sweet portion there.

(Joseph M. Scriven 1855)

DO YOU WANT TO BECOME FRIENDS WITH JESUS TOO?

Here Is What Must Happen

> If we confess our sins to Him,
> He is faithful and just to forgive
> and cleanse us from all our unrighteousness.

By now, you must be entirely confident that you cannot have fellowship with the Holy God, our Creator, the master of the universe, in any other way except through His Son Jesus. This was clearly stated in John's book: "Jesus saith unto him, I am the way, the truth, and the life: no one cometh unto the Father, but by me" (John 14:6). To be a friend of Jesus, you must first accept that Jesus died on the cross of Calvary deliberately for your sin's sake. You are instantly redeemed of every erroneous thought about Him when you feel sure of this. According to the book of Corinthians, "Therefore if any man is in Christ, he is a new creature: old things are passed away; behold, all things have become new" (2 Corinthians 5:17).

God thoroughly washes and cleans every sin and guilt recorded in your name. Don't you think that's breathtaking? Understandably, you may not have a prodigious sensation of jam-packed guilt and shame. You may not feel any physical changes right now since it is a supernatural transaction. Emotions must be trained to catch up with the spiritually influenced changes.

> When you came to Christ, you were "circumcised," but not by a physical procedure. Christ performed a spiritual circumcision—the cutting away of your sinful nature. For you were buried with Christ when you were baptized. And with Him, you were raised to new life because you trusted the mighty power of God, who raised Christ from the dead (Colossians 2:11-12 (NLT)

If you find out that your heart still meddles with a tremendous sense of guilt, it may be a great help to let your new friend (Jesus) know how sorry you feel deep inside of you by confessing any of your sins. God assured us that "if we confess our sins to Him, He is faithful and just to forgive and cleanse us from all our unrighteousness" (1 John 1:9). He also encouraged us to come to Him now so we can reason together with Him. He said, "Though your sins are like scarlet, they shall be as white as snow; though red like crimson, they shall be as wool" (Isaiah 1:18).

To crown this redemption process, we must also believe Christ rose from the dead and ascended to heaven to prepare a home for us. For this reason, we can be forgiven with the empowerment to live a holy and acceptable life before God. Only Christ can help you live a righteous life through the power of His resurrection. It will be a great pleasure before God to see you treasure this moment with a helpful prayer of determination, inviting Jesus Christ into your life. You may make your own words from the depth of your heart, but for those new to this, you may use this prayer guide as a model to begin your talk with your new friend.

Oh, Lord Jesus, I acknowledge I've been a sinner against people, myself, and God.

I clearly understand now that your death on the cross has paid for my sins.

I firmly believe that, and I love and appreciate you for it.

I'm extending to you a sincere invitation into my life to be my Lord and Savior.

I understand that I also accept eternal life by receiving you, and I shall live and reign forever in heaven with you.

From now henceforth, I want you to be my very best friend!

Dwell inside of me by your Holy Spirit. Kindly allow my body to be the temple of the Holy Spirit.

Fill me up with your Spirit, Lord Jesus! So I may do great things in your name to glorify you.

I want to know you more and find your other friends who can help me with my new friendship with you.

In Jesus name, I pray (Amen).

When you are done with your conversation with God, know He has seen and heard every word from you. And now you are a friend of Jesus! I officially welcome you into this great family. God has warned us never to be ignorant of the enemy's devices. Satan, of course, is the enemy of God and all believers. Satan is also the accuser of brethren. He is bent on doing anything to make you doubt your redemption. Don't let Satan have his way in your life.

Whether after we have breathed our last breath or if we should live until He comes, Jesus will come and take us home.

All Jesus wants you to do is tell him constantly what is going on with you. He wants you to depend so much on His name. The name of the Lord is a strong tower. The righteous run into it, and they are safe" (Proverbs 18:10). I will end this by encouraging you to cheer up. Soon, whether after we have breathed our last breath or if we should live until He comes, Jesus will come and take us home.

For the Lord Himself shall descend from heaven with a

shout, an unchanged voice, and the trump of God. The dead in Christ shall rise first. Then we who are alive and remain shall be caught up together in the clouds. We will meet the Lord in the air, and so shall we ever be with the Lord (1 Thessalonians 4:16–17). We will get to ride a cloud with a trumpet blast. We shall get to see him face to face. The joy of the whole matter is that we will have a joyful, trouble-free life and reign in heaven with the King.

From My Heart

Dear Friend,

Once again, you are now welcome into the big family. It will be a great pleasure to see you write us a letter or email us, sharing about yourself and your new friend, Jesus. We will also be glad to hear the testimony of your redemption and what the Lord has been doing in your life. We will love to see you flourish in this new relationship of yours. Thank you for your time reading this book; I am so glad I could introduce you to Christ. I pray you will derive much joy and delight in your new relationship with Jesus.

Beloved, I earnestly pray that it may be well with you in all aspects of life and that you may be in good health, just as your soul keeps thriving and prospering.

Have a great & blessed life!

Remain blessed & inspired!

Dr. Aigbefo D. Ehihi

End Notes

1. Mahzad Hojjat and Anne Moyer, *The Psychology of Friendship* (Oxford, NY: Oxford University Press, 2017), xix.
2. Mahzad Hojjat and Anne Moyer, xix.
3. Cathy Mason, "What's Bad about Friendship with Bad People?" *Canadian Journal of Philosophy* 51, no. 7 (2021): 523–534.
4. *The Psychology of Friendship: Friendship and Health*. 245.
5. Cathy Mason, "What's Bad about Friendship with Bad People?"
6. *The Psychology of Friendship: Friendship and Health*, 233.
7. Valentina Punzo, "How Crime Spreads through Imitation in Social Networks: A Simulation Model," *New Frontiers in the Study of Social Phenomena* (2016): 169–190.
8. Cathy Mason, "What's Bad about Friendship with Bad People?"
9. Ibid.
10. Cathy Mason, "What's Bad about Friendship with Bad People?"
11. Ibid.
12. Cathy Mason, "What's Bad about Friendship with Bad People?"
13. Proverbs 13:20, paraphrased.
14. II Cor. 13:33, paraphrased.
15. Lewis, C. S. (1998). *The Four Loves*. HarperCollins.
16. Ibid.

REFERENCES

Mason, Cathy. "What's Bad about Friendship with Bad People?" *Canadian Journal of Philosophy* 51, no. 7 (2021): 523–534.

Hojjat, Mahzad, and Anne Moyer. *The Psychology of Friendship*. Oxford, NY: Oxford University Press, 2017.

Wikström, P.-O. H. (2004). Crime as an Alternative: Towards a cross-level situational action theory of crime causation. In J.

McCord (Ed.), *Beyond empiricism: Institutions and intentions in the study of crime. Advances in criminological theory* (Vol. 13, pp. 1–37). New Brunswick: Transaction.

Punzo, Valentina. "How Crime Spreads through Imitation in Social Networks: A Simulation Model." *New Frontiers in the Study of Social Phenomena* (2016): 169–190.

Mason, Cathy. "What's Bad about Friendship with Bad People?" *Canadian Journal of Philosophy* 51, no. 7 (2021): 523–534.

Crosnoe, R., & Needham, B. (2004). Holism, contextual variability, and the study of friendships in adolescent development. Child development.

"Jonathan and David – A True and Lasting Friendship. The Restored Church of God, Jan. 2013. Web. 03 Oct. 2015.

Scriven, J. M. (n.d.). What a Friend We Have in Jesus. Retrieved September 03, 2015, from http://library.timelesstruths.org/ music/What a Friend We Have in Jesus/.

SPECIAL NOTE

William Franklin "Billy" Graham, Jr. is a well-known American Evangelical Christian evangelist ordained as a Southern Baptist minister.

William Henry "Bill" Gates III is a famous American business magnate, philanthropist, investor, computer programmer, and inventor.

Steven Paul "Steve" Jobs was a well-respected American entrepreneur, marketer, inventor, co-founder, chairman, and CEO of Apple Inc.

Warren Edward Buffett is a distinguished American business magnate, investor, and philanthropist.

SO MANY FRIENDS,

SO LITTLE FRIENDSHIP

Imagine a world where so-called
best friends are nothing but flakes!

AIGBEFO D. EHIHI

ABOUT THE AUTHOR

AIGBEFO D. EHIHI is a Pastor, a leader, and a Chaplain. He earned his B.Sc. in Psychology from Upper Iowa University, Master of Divinity from Regent University, and D. Min in Pastoral Counseling from Liberty University, where he is pursuing a Doctor of Education in Community Care and Counseling. Dr. Ehihi has also authored numerous inspirational articles and evangelical pamphlets. He is devoted to his divine commitment to soar humanity to greater heights through God's Word. Dr. Ehihi and his wife, Precious, have a daughter and happily work together in ministry.